T0330819

ROUTLEDGE LIBRARY EDITIONS: MARKETING

Volume 11

ADVERTISING FOR ACCOUNT HANDLERS

ADVERTISING FOR ACCOUNT HANDLERS

NIGEL LINACRE

Routledge
Taylor & Francis Group

LONDON AND NEW YORK

First published in 1988

This edition first published in 2015
by Routledge
2 Park Square, Milton Park, Abingdon, Oxon, OX14 4RN

and by Routledge
711 Third Avenue, New York, NY 10017

Routledge is an imprint of the Taylor & Francis Group, an informa business

© 1988 Nigel Linacre

British Library Cataloguing in Publication Data
A catalogue record for this book is available from the British Library

ISBN: 978-0-415-83446-9 (Set)
eISBN: 978-1-315-76199-2 (Set)
ISBN: 978-1-138-78703-2 (Volume 11)
eISBN: 978-1-315-76686-7 (Volume 11)

Publisher's Note
The publisher has gone to great lengths to ensure the quality of this reprint but points out that some imperfections in the original copies may be apparent.

Disclaimer
The publisher has made every effort to trace copyright holders and would welcome correspondence from those they have been unable to trace.

Advertising for Account Handlers

Nigel Linacre

HUTCHINSON BUSINESS
London   Melbourne   Auckland   Johannesburg

Hutchinson Business
An imprint of Century Hutchinson Ltd
62–65 Chandos Place, London WC2N 4NW

Century Hutchinson Australia (Pty) Ltd
PO Box 496, 16–22 Church Street, Hawthorn,
Victoria 3122, Australia

Century Hutchinson New Zealand Ltd
PO Box 40–086, 32–34 View Road, Glenfield,
Auckland 10, New Zealand

Century Hutchinson South Africa (Pty) Ltd
PO Box 337, Bergvlei 2012, South Africa

Photoset in 10/12pt Linotron Times
by Deltatype, Ellesmere Port, Cheshire

Printed and bound in Great Britain by
Anchor Brenden Ltd, Tiptree Essex

British Library Cataloguing in Publication Data

Linacre, Nigel
  Advertising for account handlers.
  1. Advertising   2. Advertising agencies —
  Finance
  I. Title
  659.1'068'1   HF5824

  ISBN 0–09–173589–0
  ISBN 0–09–173594–7 Pbk

Contents

Foreword

Long ago in a far-off land, I was trying to make my way as a young copywriter. One day an account handler said to me, 'I'm not going to the client with that script of yours. He'll fire us.'

I said, 'How would it be if I came with you to present it? You can always disassociate yourself and the agency from it if things turn nasty.' He was a pragmatic account handler, and he was up against a deadline, so he agreed that I should go with him.

I didn't greatly fancy my chances, but I was lucky enough to sell the script to the client. The account man shared my joy. In fact, he was very pleased that he'd persuaded me to go with him to the meeting.

On the way back to the agency, feeling expansive, he offered me a chance to take a step up the corporate ladder. 'Have you ever considered becoming an account handler?' he enquired. I thought about it for a second or two and replied, 'If I was faced with the prospect, I think I'd try and get into some other business.'

I hadn't reconsidered this view until now. Nigel Linacre makes account handling sound like the only role worth having in advertising. The job around which the agency revolves. And that's how a self-respecting account person should feel.

There are books about art direction, copy writing and media which produce this effect, but I'm not aware of one aimed at account handlers. It's rather strange that a business which considers spotting market gaps so important should have apparently overlooked this one.

However, Nigel Linacre, one of a new breed of intensely professional young account handlers, cast his eye over the bibliography of advertising, spotted the opportunity and sat down and wrote this encyclopedic handbook. In his spare time. (Traditionally, account people are incapable of speech in their leisure time due to drink or dalliance, let alone writing a book.) Having read it, I realize that for many years I have consistently undervalued the contribution account handlers make to the business. In my defence all I can say is that I am not the only copywriter to make this mistake. Robin Wight declared that account handlers weren't necessary when he started his super-star agency. But he changed his mind, and the agency hasn't looked back since.

From a copywriter's standpoint it's an easy error to fall into. You generally only see account people when they pop into your office to tell you how to do the advertising so that the client will accept it, and make their life easier. Or they sidle in to explain why they failed to sell your work and to ask you to produce a replacement. Between times they come with stick or carrot to encourage you to meet deadlines. Other than that, God only knows what they're up to. In the creative department it is generally supposed they are entertaining the client. If asked what I really thought their job was about, I would probably have said something like 'Oiling the agency machinery'.

Well, now I know what they do.

I am grateful to Nigel for putting me in the picture. I could argue with a few of his assertions about the business but I won't. After all, it isn't a science and even scientists have been known to quibble.

Perhaps he would have written a less contentious book if he had had another ten or fifteen years' experience to go on. But the fact that he has written it while he is still coming to terms with the job himself, makes it particularly valuable to people thinking about taking it on and to those already feeling their way up the lower rungs of the ladder. That is not to say it has nothing to offer the more experienced.

Many account people who have spent years working on the same account or in the same agency will find the scope of the book very stimulating. It covers every aspect of the job in the many forms it assumes in different agencies. It is packed with practical advice and check lists. It is a how-to-do-it hand book that belongs on every account handler's desk. And it should certainly be read by all those ignoramuses like me who aren't sure what account people do.

I think this book will improve the way advertising agencies go about their business.

John Salmon
November 1987
Executive Creative Director
Collett Dickenson Pearce and Partners Ltd.

Acknowledgements

Most of all, I could not have written this book without Sheila Bull, who's written more good copy for more advertisers than anyone else I know. She's also spotted more duff advertising briefs. She's nurtured the idea from its earliest stage, helped draft sections of this book and edited the rest.

I am also indebted to Deva Sagenkahn of Bird & Co for encouragement, Simon Clemmow of Gold Greenlees Trott for many suggestions, Peter Clucas of McColl for help at so many stages, Richard Collins, Eleni Papadakis and Sarah Spain of BMP Business for suggestions, Mark Dixon of Mark Dixon & Company, New York, a former colleague for much early help, Ed Floyd, an art director at WWAV for his sense of humour, Yotis Georgi of Barclays who suggested the right publisher and reviewed the text, Orlando Kimber of Heart Music For Pictures for inspiration, persistence and jingles, Vivian Linacre for unlimited enthusiasm, Richard Thoburn of Richard Thoburn Associates for so much, Nick White for publishing advice, and to Annie Cochrane, Julia Benjamin and Linda Graham for typing early, middle and later versions of this book, and Camilla St. Johnston for help with proof-reading; and especially to my wife, Sue Linacre for so much more.

Collett Dickenson Pearce, BMP Business and particularly CDP Financial Partnership have all helped in different ways. All the errors and omissions remain mine.

Chapter 1

Introduction

Is This Book for You?

This book is written for today's and tomorrow's account handlers, and all the people they deal with. It provides a close-up view of the whole advertising process.

Most people in advertising are alternately helped and frustrated by account handlers – from clients to copywriters, and from art directors to media buyers and salesmen. For them, this book will help explain a handler's point of view and motives, and so suggest effective ways to work with him.

For account handlers themselves there is the opportunity to stop and think, and to develop a point of view. Almost all account handlers can improve themselves, the author included. Good account handlers aren't born, they're made as experience takes them up the learning curve. This book might help shorten that curve, and show a few short cuts.

I must apologise to all the many talented female account handlers, clients, copywriters, planners etc. I know. The English language does not, alas, contain a pronoun that means 'he or she'. So I've settled on 'he' throughout, but *only* for ease of reading.

This is a practical book which you could keep at work within handy reach. It's as short as the subject permits and could probably be read from cover to cover in about four hours or so. In fact, it's probably best read selectively and mulled over.

How to Find Your Way Around This Book

Section I is about account handling. It starts by surveying the big picture – the world of advertising – and gradually becomes more focused as it looks at advertising agencies and how they work. It then considers what account handlers do and don't do and introduces a special member of the team: the account planner. Chapter 3 concentrates on good account handling, and in the following chapter the detail of handling advertising accounts is studied. Mostly, account handling *is* detail.

Section II concerns the creation of advertising campaigns. It starts off by interrogating the product and then considers the role of advertising. Media and creative briefings follow. Working with the creative team, reviewing their work and selling it to the clients are the subjects of the next three chapters. And buying advertising media, going into production and assessing the campaign are the final three chapters of the section.

Section III deals with all the bits and pieces, but especially with management. Supporting the campaign below the line provides a brief overview of other communications disciplines, like public relations and direct mail. Managing clients, colleagues and money are the subject of the next two chapters and some agency politics are thrown in – a brief survival course.

Meetings have a chapter all of their own. It's really about how to get more done in shorter meetings. Chapter 19 on new business includes some hints; in essence, it's about going for it.

Advertisers warrant a special, made-to-measure chapter. After all, being a good client is difficult; they are to be treasured. And Chapter 21 is about the advertising industry's value.

Chapter 22 is concerned with the best way to develop your advertising career. Learn to sell, and then some more. After all, you can't get much richer simply by working *more* hours. You need to find ways to work better.

The final chapter is a glossary of 101 terms. It helps to know exactly what they mean.

Part I
Account handling

Chapter 2

It's an ad world

Advertising is an extraordinary business – in the people it attracts, their working circumstances and the way they go about their work.

Where do advertising agencies come from? They were originally owned by the media owners to whom their first loyalty lay. They were not independent organizations. They made their money not by taking a commission in space but by trading it, or more specifically by buying space in bulk at a discount, and selling it on. Next, they started a copywriting service to encourage clients to buy their space, and soon afterwards they added design and art services.

From a legal point of view, however, an 'agency' now contracts in its own right with both clients and media owners. It is nobody's agent, in the sense of being owned by another organization. Today, agencies are independent of media and clients. Legally, they act as principals rather than agents and have separate contracts with both parties.

Inside advertising

Advertising has been defined as any piece of paid-for communication which is designed to persuade its audience. It usually involves just four groups of people: *the advertiser* who has a product which he wants to sell; *the advertising agency* which creates advertising proposals; *the media* which carry the advertising; and *the suppliers* who help the agency turn ideas into reality.

The *advertiser* owns the product which is to be promoted. He pays for the advertisements to be thought-up, produced and put into the media. Each advertiser, or client, hires and fires his agency as he wants to.

Advertisers are, of course, companies in their own right and their effectiveness sometimes appears to the agency to be constrained by internal political hurdles. The agency may typically be dealing with a *brand manager* (usually responsible for one or more products with a particular brand name), *marketing managers* (responsible for marketing a range of products) or, in some cases, a *sales manager*. The titles are endless.

These managers will usually report to directors who may, in turn, report to others. The agency's contact is only one individual in one

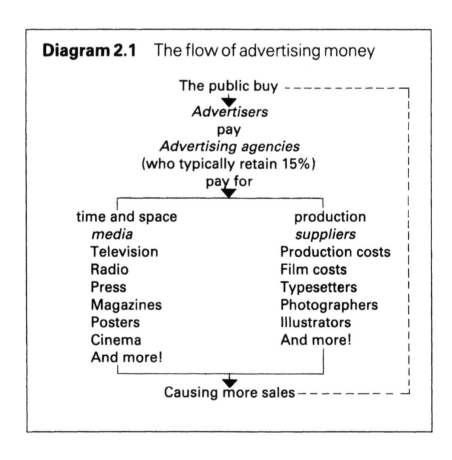

Diagram 2.1 The flow of advertising money

The public buy ─ ─ ─ ─ ─ ─ ─ ─ ─ ─ ┐
↓
Advertisers
pay
Advertising agencies
(who typically retain 15%)
pay for
↓

time and space	production
media	*suppliers*
Television	Production costs
Radio	Film costs
Press	Typesetters
Magazines	Photographers
Posters	Illustrators
Cinema	And more!
And more!	

Causing more sales ─ ─ ─ ─ ─ ─ ─ ─ ┘

department within the company, and the company's definition of its priorities may not coincide with that of the department. The advertising agency sometimes provides a shoulder for its frustrated clients to cry on.

Advertisers should know more about their products and markets than the agency, but they may well know less about advertising. Some agencies affect to adore their clients, some simply have serious business relationships with them and others don't respect them at all. In the end, however, it's the clients who call the shots.

The *media* take most of any advertiser's money – 85 per cent as a rule. The agency holds on to 15 per cent of the media expenditure as a commission, although some now agree to charge fees instead. Media have their own sales departments which compete for slices of advertising budgets. They lobby the advertisers and the agencies.

The advertising agencies

Advertising agencies are in business to create advertisements. If the agency is any good, it creates memorable advertisements which are liked by the public, add to the product's intrinsic value, and help the client's sales figures climb satisfactorily upwards. If the agency is not very good, it creates dull advertisements which go unnoticed by the public, make no difference to sales figures, and, at best, do no harm to the product. You pays your money and you takes your choice.

Within the agency, the 'account handler' is variously titled 'account executive', 'account manager' or 'account director', depending on his seniority, and how liberal his agency is at dishing

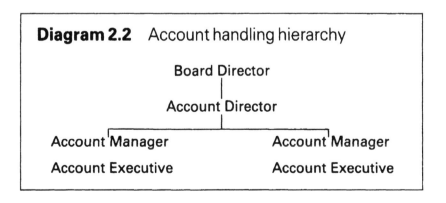

Diagram 2.2   Account handling hierarchy

Board Director

Account Director

Account Manager   Account Manager

Account Executive   Account Executive

out titles. One leading agency calls him the sales representative, or sales rep for short. The 'account' bit of the handler's title is simply derived from the fact that he looks after some of the agency's clients, each of whom has an 'account' at the agency.

Each advertising agency has several departments. A *media department* deals with the whole business of where the advertising will appear. The media people plan which medium to use and when and how, and also negotiate prices with the media. These two functions are sometimes split between 'media planners' and 'media buyers'. Alternatively, clients can use a separate company for this, known as a *media independent*, while their agency produces the advertisements.

Most large agencies have in-house *planners* or researchers. Planners are concerned with getting the agency's thinking straight before creative work is requested, as well as ensuring that the final work reflects that thinking.

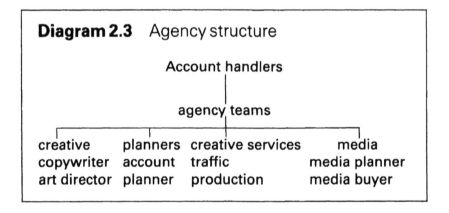

Diagram 2.3   Agency structure

		Account handlers		
		agency teams		
creative	planners	creative services		media
copywriter	account	traffic		media planner
art director	planner	production		media buyer

Advertising agencies employ *creative* teams, usually a duo of an *art director* and a *copywriter*, to produce the advertising idea, normally called a *concept*, and subsequently any pictures and words that will eventually go into the advertising. The agency can also buy these skills freelance, especially if it is particularly busy. These people are often called *creatives*.

In fact, all sorts of specialists contribute facts, thoughts, opinions and ideas before a definitive brief is written for the copywriter and art director (the creative team) whose job it is to think up the ideas that will eventually be seen by the public as finished advertisements: the single pieces of persuasion that both client and agency believe will say the right things, to the right people, at the right time, to get consumers trying or buying the product.

Many larger agencies have people responsible for ensuring that internal work is done on time and that quality control systems are applied. Usually they are called *traffic* people. Control systems often mean that work must be approved by senior staff before it can be presented to the client, and that all work must be checked. The traffic department is the nerve centre of the agency. It ensures that each brief and advertisement is correctly routed through the agency, and that everything happens according to plan. Traffic people must produce a detailed timing plan which covers all stages of production and tallies with the media plan, and they must see that it is followed.

Most agencies also employ *production* experts, who are concerned with the quality of the finished advertisements, which are normally completed outside the agency by *suppliers*, including studios and typesetting houses and, whenever necessary, directors and production companies, photographers and illustrators. The biggest agencies often have specialist TV departments to oversee the finished quality of all their TV, radio and cinema work. Agencies usually mark up outside production costs which are incurred on their clients' behalf. They mark up the net amounts by 17.65 per cent which equates to 15 per cent of the gross, or by whatever they think they can get away with.

Most agencies also have a *vouchers* department. It is its responsibility to obtain a copy of every advertisement that appears in print. It supplies the *accounts department* with the relevant newspaper or magazine, which is affixed to the agency's invoice for the space. Some advertisers refuse to pay unless they receive a voucher copy. They want to see for themselves that the advertisement has appeared and to check the quality of the printing. If the client's product looks cheap and nasty because of poor printing, he is entitled to an apology, a reduction in the bill, or a free repeat appearance if the reproduction was really poor.

Larger agencies often put traffic people and production people into one department. Its function is to help provide the right environment and working habits for good advertising to be created. It is usually called a *Creative Services* department.

Agencies do not keep photographers, illustrators, musicians, film directors and producers on their books. Although most agencies use these kinds of people regularly, they will choose which individuals to use on each campaign. This helps produce the best effect each time. Most of these people work with lots of different advertising agencies.

The tenth biggest advertising agency in Britain employs only about 250 people, including account handlers, art directors, copywriters, media buyers and planners, production and traffic people, and secretaries. These people are on the payroll because their services are required more or less constantly.

Two honest points of view

Some advertising agencies will tell you that all agencies are the same. Others will tell you that they are different. What is the truth?

They are almost all the same inasmuch as they produce advertising and they hire account handlers, creative, media, planning and production people. Almost all of them use briefing forms which cover the same sort of ground and they produce concepts, storyboards and media schedules amongst other things.

However, beyond these basics, advertising agencies do go about their work in different ways. They have their own goals, philosophies and people. This makes some of them better at creating new campaigns while others are better at developing old ones. Some are safe, others take risks. Some concentrate on thinking and others on style. And I'm thinking only of the biggest agencies.

Agencies that tell you there isn't much difference between them are telling you the truth as they see it. They can't see any difference. The agencies which tell you they are different can see a difference.

What account handlers don't do

Advertising is a very public business. Yet the advertising process is quite mysterious – especially the role of the advertising agency creature called the account handler. The importance of account handling itself is severely under-rated by many, not least by the account handlers themselves. It's easy to explain why.

They don't write the advertisements; the copywriter does this. Nor do they think up how the radio or TV commercial, press advertisement, poster or whatever will look; the art director does that. The copywriter and art director work together to create the advertising idea. And they both report to a creative director who supervises and can veto their work. So account handlers don't *create* advertising.

Except in the smallest of agencies, account handlers don't plan, negotiate with or book media. The advertising agency's media department does this, employing media managers or specialist media planners who are complemented by media buyers.

Nor do account handlers see to the production of the advertising – how the creative team's basic idea is translated into a finished advertisement. Production experts are employed to do this. And account handlers don't undertake much research. This is usually supervised by account planners and briefed out of the agency to specialist research companies. And traffic experts, often allied to their agency's production department, see the agency's work through from the beginning of each assignment to the appearance of the advertisement.

Some agencies find it difficult to define exactly what an account handler does. Some of the account handler's functions are easily caricatured. He's the smart man (or woman) within the agency, the 'suit'. He's the person who carries the agency's bags and lunches the clients. He's the agency's salesperson, but he's very much more. Some account handlers see their own work in such simple terms, and they rely on intuition and style without trying to learn their craft. Most of these people wouldn't think of account handling as a skill.

Some have been known to earn the nickname, 'account fumbler'. Yet all advertising agencies employ account handlers and some small agencies employ nothing but account handlers and buy the other services freelance. Without account handlers, you simply don't have an advertising agency. Without *good* account handlers, you simply don't have a *good* agency.

Added value from account planners

At most big British agencies, the account management function is divided into two. At these agencies there are account planners whose job is to ensure that the advertising works, and account handlers whose job is to serve their clients' needs. Clearly, the tasks overlap. Clients are more likely to be satisfied with an agency if the advertising is working. And they won't keep their account at the agency indefinitely if the advertising doesn't work.

So while the account handler tries to understand what the client needs, the account planner begins to develop an understanding of the needs of the advertiser's *consumers*. They'll probably work on this together. A planner's work usually includes testing advertising propositions at an early stage amongst groups of consumers to see what is likely to work.

The account planner will study the client's brief and discuss it with the handler. He'll usually be keen to analyse existing market data: everything from sales figures to market reports, usage and attitude surveys and awareness tracking studies. He may decide that more research is necessary and recommend that it is commissioned. Upon agreement, he'll see that it is carried out. The main objective of this work is to fill out the account handler's picture of what is going on in the marketplace and what the role of the advertising should be: exactly what should we be saying to whom?

If a number of advertising routes remain open, the handler and planner might have a creative team produce some rough advertising ideas exemplifying a number of possibilities and carefully test them amongst consumers either in group discussions or in one-to-one depth interviews, to see which routes provoke the most favourable response. This is sometimes called *concept research*, and the boards on which the advertising ideas are mounted are called *concept boards* or *reactor boards*.

Usually, the account handler gets his planner's agreement to the resulting advertising brief before he can give it to the creative team. And in most planning-orientated agencies he'll need the planner's approval before he can take the resulting creative work to his client. The account planner will ask whether the work fulfils the advertising strategy, i.e. is it saying what the agency wants to get across? He will also ask whether the consumer will get the point, i.e. will he understand it? Here again research may be useful. This creative work might be tested amongst groups of consumers too. If the work survives the research it runs unamended, otherwise it is either refined or binned.

Although some of the advantages of research are discussed later in this book, a word of warning is appropriate at this stage. The account handler should use research to extend his judgement, not to substitute for it. Some of the campaigns that researched badly have been among the most successful. Judgement comes first: but if the handler wants to override research, he had better be right!

The account planner might also help sell creative work to the client by explaining how and why the advertising will work for the brand. (And by agreeing to research the proposed work, if the client *won't* buy it immediately.)

Before the advertising campaign runs, the account planner will be responsible for any final pre-testing of the relatively finished work. He will also help assess the advertising campaign's effectiveness, consider whether the advertising's objectives are being realized (and if not why not), and decide whether the advertising needs further development.

Anyway what are you trying to do when you start advertising for a particular client? More than just running a single advertisement, or even a series of them, you should be aiming to produce a campaign.

All the advertisements in any one campaign must have the same advertising objective. They'll aim to create and reinforce the same positioning for your client's product in the consumer's mind. The advertisements in any one campaign must also feel the same, if they are going to encourage the consumer to feel the same way about the product. This could be achieved in many different ways.

Usually, the advertisements *look* similar: either the same thing happens in each advertisement, or the same elements feature. In either case, your product must be treated similarly. If you are going to send it up in one commercial, you must send it up in every commercial. Similarly in newspapers, magazines and posters you should keep to one typeface and one format. You can also use a similar style of words. They might have the same structure, a similar pace and a consistent tone of voice.

Advertising has to work hard to get noticed and even harder to get remembered and acted upon. So the most important thing of all is that any *one* campaign is about just one idea. And the more single-minded you can be about that, the more powerful your client's campaign will be. More about this later.

What do account handlers do?

Account handlers are involved in virtually every part of the advertising process. As an account handler, you work with everyone, from the client's marketing department to the representatives of the media in which the advertising appears.

You'll take briefs from clients and guide and motivate your agency's departments. You'll help judge every piece of the agency's work and sell it to your client. It's the handler's job to bring out the best in the client and also in his agency colleagues. (None of them has a corresponding responsibility to him.)

You see the agency's work through all its stages, from briefing to release to the media and appearance. Your clients and your agency colleagues believe the buck stops with you. And it usually does: you are the fall guy when things go wrong, and just one of the heroes when things go right.

True, you don't usually write the advertisements or provide their visual appearance, nor do you undertake the research nor, often, develop the strategy. You don't negotiate with the media or produce the finished advertisements. But a good account handler will help copywriters and art directors, planners, media buyers and production experts to be successful in their work. You'll prompt both inspiration and perspiration. If you can point your people in profitable directions, their work should be up to scratch, and you can do your level best to sell it to your client. You are a jack of all trades and a master of salesmanship. You run your clients and use the agency's resources to their best effect.

Moreover, account handlers often start the ball rolling by winning the business, a subject which is dealt with in another section of this book.

How can you do your work well? As a good account handler, you believe all your team's work is under your control, even though it doesn't always turn out that way. You feel responsible for everything that the agency does on your accounts. You'll pass on all credit and shoulder any blame. You won't excuse your own actions when things go wrong and you'll always believe you can be successful, however often you seem to be proved wrong. You will never allow agency politics or client hierarchies to interfere with the potential of a good piece of creative work.

You never assume anything and always check that what was promised to you is in fact being done. You won't allow other people to let you or your client down. You're an effective motivator and a manager of people, a devil's advocate and a salesman. You're a master of detail, but you won't let details master you. You are not naturally neurotic, and you always retain a sense of humour.

When you're with agency departments you represent the client's interest, and when you're with the client you represent the agency and sell its work and its point of view. You can read your clients like an open book. You'll rely on your own judgement, though you'll always be learning. You'll be willing to be led until the natural time arrives when you lead the agency. If you're still in the advertising business by the time you're forty, you're usually running an agency or at the top of a large tree with a very important title.

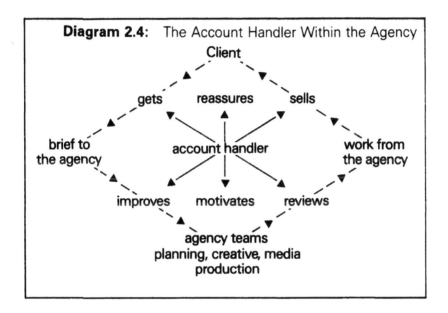

Diagram 2.4: The Account Handler Within the Agency

Handling check

As an account handler, you don't:

1 Come up with the advertising idea
2 Write the headline
3 Create the pictures
4 Design the advertisement
5 Research the advertising idea
6 Write the copy
7 Decide where to put it
8 Negotiate with the media
9 Produce the finished advertisement
10 Send out the agency invoices

(although you will manage and probably influence the whole process)

But you'll probably
1   Go and get the business
2   Take all your client's calls
3   Marshall the agency's resources
4   Motivate the agency
5   Agree the purpose of the advertising
6   Help create the proposition
7   Sell your agency's work
8   Oversee production
9   Keep your agency's work profitable
10 Keep your agency team happy
11 Keep your client happy
(although you will need help if you are to succeed)

Chapter 3

What flavour is account handling?

Advertising agencies are unusually stimulating places to work and the account handler's job is arguably the most exciting and varied of the lot. It has momentous highs and lows.

As an account handler you deal with a tremendous variety of people and businesses, each with its own culture. You can get right inside their problems and opportunities, just like a corporate psychiatrist. And you get to study consumers too, plus all those weird and wonderful people within the advertising business.

Then there is the intellectual challenge of helping to solve product, marketing and communication problems in order to satisfy consumer wants better. There's also the satisfaction of seeing your work through from briefing to appearance in a fairly short period of time, typically ranging from a month to a year. And the creative environment is a bonus.

There's the excitement of the high-wire artist. You're continually trying to achieve great things, but there's always the danger that you'll put a foot wrong or that your clients will leave the agency anyway. As they sometimes do. There's the thrill of competition for business and the drama of presentations to clients, today's and the future's. There are so many opportunities to perform, and it's a high-profile glamorous industry.

There's temper and temperament, frustration and disappointment and continuing tension. In the advertising world, what goes up must come down, at least until Saatchis came along! And you are only as good as your last advertisement. There's farce too. Every day there's something or someone to laugh at, and it definitely helps if you can laugh at yourself.

Account handling is not a business for people who are already insecure. It's an occupation for people who are self-confident communicators, with at least a hint of charisma and some brainpower. Combine this mixture with personal sensitivity, attention to detail and an appetite for interesting work, and you should have a good account handler. The rest can be learnt, although it often isn't.

As an account handler, it's very easy to lose hold of your work as so many others attempt to take control. Worse still is to get out of step with the things that you need to get done. If you get out of kilter you may never catch up. Once you lose hold of the reins, you've lost control of that particular horse.

And you can get stretched or squeezed as your agency leaves your client behind or vice versa, or they head for a confrontation with you in the middle. Some account-handling strategies are reminiscent of a Buster Keaton character. He sought to retrieve his cow from a strip between the Confederate and Yankee lines. So he set off carrying a flag which showed the federal flag to the south and the Yankee flag to the north. All was peaceful until the wind changed when Keaton was a few yards short of the cow. Then both sides were out to get him.

Most account handlers would rather risk the wrath of their colleagues than that of their clients, even though their colleagues may hit them harder. Account handlers feel secure only if their clients are happy. If clients are unhappy, hysteria and depression are held in check only by fear.

Most account handlers put a lot of emotional energy into their work and live their life to the full. The lifestyle is fast, fun and expensive. Salaries are anything but guaranteed. They start out fairly low. So many people want to start in advertising, and some really would start for nothing (though few agencies are willing to be seen paying absolutely nothing). Thereafter, it's up to you. Salaries tend to be individually negotiated. So, how good a negotiator are you?

Every kind of handler

Account handlers exist at all levels of ability and seniority. And the two often don't go together. To explain what each kind of account handler did at every stage in this book would be tedious. So, in order to treat them as though they were the same, some words of explanation about the different kinds of account handler are necessary now.

Good account handlers delegate to the limit, so the action can be pretty thin at the top. At most agencies, one or another board director has some overall responsibility for each of the agency's accounts. As there are usually many more accounts in an agency than there are board directors, his involvement in each account is likely to be very modest. He might sign off each creative brief (or the agency's managing director might do so), and he might see each advertising concept and be required to approve it before the client sees it. His main concern is that these accounts contribute to the well-being of the agency. For as long as they do, the agency's board need not be involved collectively, excepting, perhaps, with the agency's very biggest accounts.

Each account team is headed up by the *account director*. He is in charge of the account within the agency and is responsible for its success or failure. He has almost unlimited responsibility for what happens to his accounts. He is likely to focus his involvement on the main issues and try to steer the account towards success for both agency and advertiser. He'll have good antennae. Like the board director, he'll approve the creative and media briefs and work, but he'll also attend any account reviews and sort out any problem areas. He'll supervise the other account handlers just as much as he feels necessary. He is likely to attend any major meetings with his clients, especially when they are fielding senior personnel.

Day to day, the account is run by its *Account Manager* or *Account Supervisor*. The two titles seem to be synonymous. He is constantly making decisions about how the agency's work should be done, and whom to involve on the account. Account managers are involved in virtually everything that happens on their accounts. Indeed, whenever an agency short-circuits its account handling system by cutting out its account manager, it's probably heading for trouble. Account managers know their accounts inside out.

The *account executive* is responsible for doing the work, and acting on his colleagues' judgement.

Account handlers usually try to develop an expertise in at least one kind of advertising or product area, like fast-moving consumer goods (fmcg) or 'white goods' or 'brown goods', or financial and business products which until recently were a poor relation of fmcg on account of their relatively small budgets and conservative tastes. Tastes change.

How to handle resources

Are you able to organize other people? Your main tasks are to manage your account team and keep its work on an even keel, and to keep the client happy. It's a difficult management job.

It means knowing what you want from them, and how to get it. To start with, they've got to know what you expect. Otherwise they'll guess, and they might guess wrong. Explanations are necessary on two levels. You need to explain exactly what you expect from people task by task. Incomplete explanations usually lead to incomplete or irrelevant work. And you need to explain to people what you expect them to achieve in the long term. Americans call this goal-setting.

One of the most frustrating things in advertising is to have a task changed while you are in the throes of doing it. First you are briefed, then you start work and make some progress, and then the job changes. You are wasting time. Unfortunately, many account handlers are guilty of this crime. You need not be amongst them.

It's useful to give your creative people an insight into how you are running the account and what is going on; you'll probably get better work if they feel involved. And they might even appreciate your handling. Remember that with creative people the most important thing is that their advertisements run un-tampered with as far as possible. If they believe that all your efforts are towards selling their work, they usually work harder and better on your accounts. (But only for as long as you keep on selling their work intact.)

One technique that is underused in some agencies is thanking people for their work, and congratulating them when you're successful. Everyone enjoys praise. Equally, you've got to be clear with your colleagues when they get it wrong. If you don't tell them, maybe no-one else will, in which case they'll probably go on doing it wrong. It's important to do this clearly and sensitively. And let them know that you still believe in their abilities.

21 Handling habits

There are some fairly commonplace habits that every account handler would do well to avoid. And other habits that are worth fully developing.

Always deliver what you've promised. A reputation for reliability means that your word counts. It also necessitates thinking ahead and not promising what your agency can't deliver.

Never make excuses. Your agency's problems aren't the client's problems and there is no reason why he should be interested in them. Failure permits no excuses: either succeed or be honest about it.

Always own up and apologise, then take it on the chin. You'll feel better about it, and your client will feel vindicated. If a client is angry, you have to deal with it; no-one else will. And if you can let a client be angry without losing your cool (or making excuses), you can deepen the agency–client relationship. Is it surprising that intemperate people tend to like people they can be intemperate with?

Never assume anything. This should be written up in every agency in letters three feet high. Account handlers are paid so that everyone else can make assumptions. You authorize the agency's assumptions only after you've checked them out first.

Always deliver the agency's work within the time agreed. In order to achieve this, you'll need to enjoy the respect of your colleagues, and a certain amount of luck. A poor sense of timing has lost many advertising accounts. However, since creating advertising takes time, you've a responsibility to allow enough of it to complete each task.

Never lie to clients, colleagues or yourself. Account handlers are paid to be relied upon. Your word is your greatest asset. And no amount of wishful thinking will get you out of a scrape.

Sometimes people tell you lies. Usually about why work is needed, or when it's needed. But they often get found out. And then their word doesn't count for so much, which is a shame, and entirely their own fault.

There can be a temptation to agree with others even when you don't. My advice is to say nothing when you are unsure, but to speak out whenever you have no doubts. At the same time, you must listen to others and if the agency wants to go in a particular direction, either buckle under or get out. Just don't rock the boat, it might sink.

So what do you do if the agency wants you to sell work that you don't believe is right? One option is that a colleague sells it on your behalf. But if you do have to sell it, there is no contradiction. You can point to its strengths and you can say, truthfully, that 'this is the work that we (the agency) want you to buy'.

Moreover, until you are directing an account you should confine yourself to talking about the agency's views. Stick to the third person (when selling work you don't believe is right).

It's important to be loyal to your clients and your colleagues, whether or not they may seem to you to deserve your loyalty. In particular, you should never blame your client for errors that you could have avoided. Stand by your client, and he will probably stand by you. Rubbish him, and so will the rest of the agency! Make yourself responsible wherever possible.

And you shouldn't criticize your colleagues unless they report to you. Even then, you should try to avoid criticizing them, explicitly or implicitly, in front of the client. Or insensitively. Your clients are dealing with the whole agency, not a part of it.

Equally, never gossip at other people's expense. Agencies are small places, and the word gets round pretty quickly. An account director once moaned about his boss to a young lady he met at a wedding. Guess who she was? He was in big trouble.

Look on every agency failure as being your own. Then see what you can do about it. Moaning is simply unacceptable in advertising agencies. It doesn't help anyone, least of all you.

Handling check

1 Never promise what you can't deliver, however great the pressure. And always deliver what you've promised.
2 Never make excuses. Failure permits no excuses, success requires no explanations.
3 Never fail to own up. They'll feel better and so will you.
4 Never lie to clients. Sooner or later you forfeit their trust.
5 Never lie to colleagues. You forfeit their trust even sooner.
6 Never lie to yourself. Who are you kidding?
7 Never commit the agency, unless you're sure it's right to do so.
8 Never deliver work late. Always aim to deliver it early.
9 Never deliver yourself to a meeting late. Be slightly early.
10 Never ask for a meeting unless you know what you want out of it.

11 Never say what you don't believe, but always listen to others.
12 Never put your name to sloppy written work. Check all your work until there are no errors.
13 Never stop learning.
14 Never waste your colleagues' or clients' time. Keep your written work succinct and your meetings short.
15 Never blame clients for your mistakes. You end up believing yourself.
16 Never criticize a colleague in front of the client.
17 Never forget to do your work. If you can't do it immediately, either write it down or perfect your memory.
18 Never moan or winge.
19 Never gossip unkindly about others. It gets back to people surprisingly quickly.
20 Never assume anything. Account handlers are not paid to make assumptions.
21 Never pass the buck. Every agency failure is the account handler's failure.

Chapter 4

How to master the everyday detail

Manage yourself

Efficiency begins at home. Account handlers must be able to organize themselves so that they can respond quickly as well as take initiatives. Either way, organizing time and identifying priorities is critical, and this calls for planning.

An account handler who doesn't take charge of his own day is like a cork bobbing on the ocean. So many people can make claims on your time. And *sometimes* you must respond immediately. As an account handler, you need to superimpose your own goals on your day.

You must develop each client. Account executives may simply embrace their account director's point of view, at least until they know better.

Advertising agencies are great places for making work, some of it unnecessary. All too often, work expands to fill the time available. Good account handlers will seek to minimize the time it takes them to do each task well, and then achieve something extra with the time gained. You should also delegate wherever possible.

Handling check

1 Do you know at the beginning of each day what you want to achieve?
2 Do you measure your performance in achieving these goals?
3 Do you plan your day? (Or do events control you?)
4 Do you have weekly and monthly goals for your accounts and yourself? (Or do you expect to be successful anyway?)
5 In what ways are you being *least* efficient?
6 Which aspects of your work are taking you longer than they should?
7 What better working habits have you seen others use? Why don't you use them?

How to control your day

Imagine that you are bombarded with requests for action throughout the day – from clients, media, creative and traffic, as well as other account handlers. How can you stay afloat?

How much thought do you give to your working habits? I believe that many account handlers waste most of their time. Account handling involves doing things, and especially doing the right things. A junior account handler ought to work hard at ensuring that he *achieves* things throughout each working day.

You might begin your day with a list of things you want to achieve (your goals). And a note of the things you know you are going to have to do in order to achieve them. One way to do this is to keep a notebook. It's more difficult to lose than individual sheets of paper, it's more private, and if it's pocket-sized, you can keep it with you. If you use a pocket diary as a notebook, you can write down each task you want to do on the day you'll need to do it, even if that is some time ahead. So, if the creative work is due next Friday, you simply make a note on next Friday's date to chase the work. Then you won't get caught unawares. You'll also have a good idea of when you are going to be busy, and you can schedule your appointments accordingly.

This has two distinct advantages. First, you have a guaranteed reminder of each job. Second, you don't have to waste mental energy trying to *remember* things, freeing more time to *think* about new things.

An Action List

Priority Action List 1.2.88

Calls
John re schedule
Mike re copy comments
Hamish: to keep in contact
Sarah re trade promotion
Matthew re his priorities

Dictate
Contact report on BB
Letter to W re timing plan
Media brief
Congratulatory letter to B

See
Creative re progress on C
Traffic for time on proofs
Proofs

Read
Research report
Credentials document

Tasks can be grouped together so that, for example, all the items to be discussed with a particular client can be covered in one call. You can even estimate the time each task will take, and budget time accordingly, reviewing progress during the day. (This approach allows you to see exactly where you're spending time.)

After you've drawn up the list, it's time to start implementing it. And the best time for an account handler to start work is *before* your colleagues and clients do so. If you start the day after them, you may never catch up!

At the end of each day, or more frequently, you should review your action list. It can be helpful to make a first draft of tomorrow's tasks at the end of the preceding day.

On the 'phone

Account handling includes selling the agency by phone. How should you handle client phone calls? Like chess games, they have openings, middles and end games. You can start your calls with the 'Hello, how are you?' line, which shows interest in your client and also gives him a chance to focus his mind on you. His response will provide a clue as to what frame of mind he's in before you decide how to handle the conversation.

Each call needs a structure to avoid becoming untidy and inconclusive. You are more likely to have a successful call if you let the client know, at the outset, what part you want him to play in it. You should set the terms of the call. For example, in calling a client:

a) John, I just wanted to go over our priorities for the day (week) and check what we are each expecting from one another . . . have you got five minutes?

This approach sets you up to go through what you intend to deliver and when, setting the client's mind at ease. This call might save him wondering just what you are up to and calling you. (By calling him, you may get crossed off his action list.) Once you have been through your items, you can ask whether there is anything else on the client's mind, so that he can notify you of anything up his sleeve, in which case you adjust your action plan accordingly. Or, as another example:

b) Andy, I wanted to let you know what our production schedule is looking like and to check out how you are doing with copy approval. I know we have plenty of time in hand, but you know as well as I do how easily it gets eaten away. We both want to avoid last-minute panics like (name the last horror you both went through).

This is a more specific approach. You can get the client on your side when you update him on some of your success (or difficulties) and he can also see that you are managing him by pressing for progress. It is almost always worthwhile taking the initiative and letting him know that you are on top of the situation:

c) Have you got a few minutes . . . we need to talk briefly about media for the regional campaign, last week's production schedules and your view on the nationals, plus one or two more things.

This opening makes it unlikely that your client will cut you off midway through the long call. If he doesn't have the time then, he will probably say so, and you can fix another time to talk.

In the middle of the call, it's very important to let the client talk, preferably at least as much as you, and get his reaction to what you are saying, along with the reasoning behind it. Depending on the nature of the assignment, and how opinionated the client is, it may be necessary to explore his opinion on each point. If he does have a problem, you should attempt to find out by asking so-called 'open-ended probes', i.e. questions that can't be answered with a simple 'yes' or 'no'. For example, 'How is it all going?' rather than 'Is everything going well?'

After all, you know your own views, but you probably don't know his. The more you can get him to describe his point of view, the more likely you are to be able to respond in an appropriate way. This needn't always mean getting the agency into line with the client's views. It often means developing the client's views towards the agency's position.

Sometimes you have to be quick on your feet. I remember once producing a press advertisement in a hurry, without the help of an art director. (Yes, this can happen, even at good agencies, especially in emergencies.) The copy had been approved and a proof of the setting was faxed to the client. We were up against it, were short of resources and had no time.

Let's call the client Bill. He's a direct no-nonsense American. The conversation went like this: 'Hi Bill, what do you think of the ad?' 'I think it's a pile of ****,' said Bill. 'That's what I admire,' I said, 'instant decision-making. Okay, now let's agree what we are going to do to improve it.' We each made some suggestions. The next proof was approved a few hours later, and the advertisement appeared satisfactorily.

Each call needs to end with an agreement. At minimum: 'Well, let us think about that and come back to you tomorrow with a recommend-ation' or 'Right, it's up to us to give you a timing plan on this.'

A postscript may be appropriate, for example, 'How is every-thing *else* going?' This will enable you either to find out about something else that is on his mind, or to lighten the tone of the conversation through a happy and positive response.

At the end of each call you can update your action list by crossing through the call items. (But you'll probably have to reinstate some of them elsewhere on your list. Advertising work tends to build its own momentum.)

Since phone calls are a particular kind of task, requiring specialized handling skills and a particular frame of mind, one efficient way to get through them can be to allocate yourself a daily phone-call period. You might, for instance, make most of your outgoing calls between 9.30 and 10.00 a.m. each day, always appreciating that you may not get through all of them.

On paper

Keep your written work brief. Many advertising agencies get bogged down in paperwork. And when there's too much of it, it simply doesn't get read.

Once you've drafted a piece of work, make a habit of going over it with a pencil and rubber and crossing out every unnecessary word. The same goes for your dictation. Keep this up until your first drafts are perfect!

You might find that the best place to get your written work done is outside office hours, at home or on the train. This out-of-office habit maximizes the time you have available to see *people* during working hours. But you may not get to *leave* the agency in time to do evening work.

One fast way to get written work done in the office is to dictate, while your secretary types straight into the word processor. Most people can talk quicker than they can write. This way, briefs, letters and memos can be printed off almost the minute your dictation is finished!

Your output is likely to include different kinds of writing. Internal documents include:

a) *Creative briefs* asking for creative work to be done, describing the task and providing the necessary information in a concentrated form. (See Chapter 7 on briefing.)
b) *Media briefs* asking for media work in the same way (also described elsewhere in this book)
c) *Estimate requests* asking for a quotation for a particular production job.
d) *Agendas* for internal and external meetings.
e) *Meeting notes* or 'contact reports' following meetings. They describe what was agreed at a client meeting and who is now to do what, often with initials of people at the right-hand margin of the

Contact report

Client:	The Company
Meeting held at:	In the Moon
Present:	Alastair Addison, Mark Dixon, Bruce MacFarlane, Camilla St Johnston, Mike Wilmot
On:	29 January 1988

The Company's springtime assault

Wherever possible, agency will have 2 days to translate client's brief into an advertising *brief*; a further day to see and brief the creative team; a working week to create a *concept* for internal review, following which either more work may be needed or a presentation meeting will be fixed; 2 days for client approval; 4 days for construction of *copy* for internal review and 2 days for its approval; up to a week for *illustration* and/or photography and one day for a first proof of *setting* with corrections following. This means planning advertising *five weeks* ahead of appearance.

Client will support agency's media buying approach and will maximize flexibility. International campaign will appear in *Times* and *Observer* this weekend, and in *Sunday Telegraph* next weekend in 33cm × 5 columns sizes. Agency should book *Telegraph* (same size) the following three Saturdays at £8,580 each.

Agency's total net media budget for Jan.–March 1988 is £200,000 including the approx. £27,000 already spent.

Client will confirm the exact (April) launch date of the *new product* and has authorized agency to book pages on the first weekend, 28cm × 4 columns or similar on the 2nd weekend, and 33cm × 5 columns In the 3rd and final launch weekend in *Telegraph*. We may also run a small tease the week before. Agency has a free hand on other media up to £100,000 net on media including £20,000 on retailers for *this* campaign. Agency will provide provisional media schedules.

Distribution: As above, plus Peter Clucas, Richard Collins, Sue Farish, Vivian Thornton.

text wherever people are asked to do something, plus a note on who was at the meeting and a distribution list for the contact report itself.

f) *Status reports* regularly itemize campaigns and other work the agency currently has in hand, their current state of play, and expected actions by client and agency for each account. An imaginary example is shown below.

g) *Memoranda* either recording some facts which should be shared

---

Status report

ANOTHER FICTITIOUS COMPANY'S STATUS REPORT

	ACTION
RESEARCH Recruitment in hand. Fieldwork to commence w/e 18 July.	Research Company
CREATIVE DEVELOPMENT Agency developing new concept for 30″ TV commercial in the light of research findings. New range of press advertisements presented to client on 7.1.88 and discussed at meeting on 11.1.88. Four are approved for development.	Agency w/c 11.1.88
CURRENT ACTIVITY i) TV 30-second commercial on air in Anglia and TVS.	
ii) *Radio* New commercial on air, Capital Radio from 1.1.88 until further notice.	Agency/ Client 7.1.88
MEDIA Media strategy document (Jan–July 1988) with client for approval.	Client asap
MISCELLANEOUS Agency/Research Company to meet supervisors. Next meeting: Tuesday 15 January, 4 p.m. at client.	Agency 15.1.86

between client and agency, or recording a particular proposal which might also be made orally.

h) *Drafts* of any of the items above or below for comment by colleagues.

For people outside the agency, your work is likely to include:

a) *Letters* which might introduce the agency, or make a particular proposal or request, solicit information or simply be the agency's public record of a set of facts. Or thank someone.

You'll find lots of opportunities to write thank-you letters. You should write after every lunch which you don't pay for, and even after most of those which you do! These letters should be crisp and to the point. But you should make them personal and individual. A 'Thank you so much for lunch today' looks standard without the addition of a line or two pertinent to your conversation.

b) *Proposal documents* for current clients and prospects. These usually accompany and elaborate upon an oral presentation. They are written to record the agency's point of view, and should be drafted once the agency's thinking is complete.

c) *Estimates and invoices.* You should supply your client with an estimate of the cost of each production job before authorizing its go-ahead, unless timing constraints dictate otherwise. Production estimates allow you to see how much a job will cost your client. The resulting price might encourage you to try doing the job in a different and cheaper way.

Your client's agreement to an estimate means you are almost certain to be paid. You have to decide whether you can rely on his verbal clearance, or whether you need written approval. If in doubt, you can put an oral approval in writing by doing a contact report of the telephone call. Unless you are trying to hide something, you've nothing to lose from breaking down each total cost into individual items and showing how each sum mounts up. Prices are valuable pieces of information, not things to be hidden or to cause embarrassment.

Providing you've done an estimate, invoicing is fairly straight-forward. In the agencies I have known, all the costs on each job are kept together in what is usually called a job bag. The job bag contains each production order to each supplier. These are subsequently matched up against their invoices. Any estimates and briefs are kept in the job bag too. And each job has a number which is used by suppliers when referring their invoices to the agency.

Once you believe a job is finished and you want to invoice the advertiser, or even if it isn't but you want to invoice him on costs to date, you get the job bag out. It normally spends its life in the agency's production department while the job is going on, before moving on to the agency's accounts department when the job is completed and you ask them to close the job bag.

The sooner you invoice your client, the sooner the agency can be paid for its work. Unissued bills cost most agencies a fortune. That's why some agencies issue invoices for half of the approved production costs before incurring any costs themselves, with the balance payable on completion.

Invoices received should match the agency's production orders. Wherever you've a spare order, you're short of at least one invoice. And an invoice without an order may be in the wrong bag. You'll need to check it out.

All in all, invoices should tally with the agency's initial estimate. You'll need to be aware of the reasons for any variations. Production invoices should cite the approved estimate and clearly explain the reasons for any variation from the estimate. If you don't do this, you'll usually find your client will query the invoice, and that holds up payment to the agency.

Additionally, you will send clients *finished versions* of work which are also distributed within the agency. These include contact and status reports, and advertising briefs and estimates.

As I've said, you owe it to your colleagues and clients to keep your written work brief. But what do you do if you're getting bogged down in other people's paperwork? When you receive it, decide whether you must react immediately or whether it can keep overnight. If you need to make an immediate response, will some handwritten notes in the margin of the note suffice as an immediate return? Or can you deal with it in one short phone call?

If you have more time, you can put the paperwork straight into your briefcase for review outside office hours.

Some account handlers leave work lying around on their desks either because they like clutter, or because they like to look busy. Don't do it unless you want to look disorganized. If the work requires you to take action, do it immediately if you can. Failing that, make a note of it on your appropriate action list.

A meeting of minds

Advertising meetings should be used to take decisions or develop thinking. They're vital because advertising is a team effort. Meetings are a big part of agency life. Meetings are an everyday occurrence. Whether they achieve very much depends on how well they are organized and how they are handled.

Organization is normally the account handler's job. Obviously, all meetings need a definite starting time, and a venue which must be entered in relevant diaries, and they *should* always start on time. Nothing is worse than sitting waiting for others, and nothing is more impolite than to be habitually late. Meetings also need a finishing time (you may need to fix your next appointment or commit yourself to finishing another piece of work by a particular time). The *relevant* people need to be present. Meetings also need an agenda itemizing subject matter, specified in advance. It's amazing how many meetings don't have this.

Apart from the subject matter, you really should know what you want to get out of the meeting. If you know what you want, you are much more likely to get it. Meetings can be most fruitfully used to allow minds to interact; to get opinions aired; to come to decisions. So get relevant information distributed in advance. You don't want valuable meeting-time wasted absorbing information.

After a productive meeting, the participants go away with a sense of purpose and achievement. They are clear about the next steps to be taken. They feel they have contributed to positive action. There's nothing like a good meeting for making people feel everyone's on the same wavelength. (As indeed, after a good meeting, they will be.)

Meetings where participants need to absorb large quantities of information are different. (Product briefing sessions, say, or research debriefs.) The more information, and the more people who attend, the less the likelihood of its being a decision-taking meeting. So treat it as an information session that requires a small follow-up decision meeting attended by only the relevant people.

You should make a note of decisions as they are made, and cover exactly what has been decided and who will do it. You should notice when nothing has been decided, or when a decision has been fudged. A fudged decision cannot be written down in an unfudged way.

Always interject and ask what is going to be done. This approach also means that a minute of the meeting is drafted by the time the meeting ends and, providing there is secretarial resource, it can be immediately typed and dispatched.

Meeting notes should be less than one page long unless the decisions cannot be described any more economically. It might be that a meeting note as such is unnecessary. For example, a meeting on production or a new business prospect meeting might best be followed by an agreed timetable showing what will be done, by what date and by whom.

Unplanned meetings

Most things that crop up in advertising just won't wait. Usually, the state of play of each client's account keeps moving during the day, causing you to make contact at short notice with clients and the agency's departments.

It's best to begin these spontaneous meetings gently. You are likely to be disrupting someone else's work and you could be very unwelcome. Don't charge in. Ask how they are. Ask if they've got a minute. Explain that something has cropped up. Then tell them what you need and see how they respond.

If the job can wait and it's difficult for them to do it right now, let them take their time (but make sure you do agree a definite completion time). This will help next time you have a job that really can't be delayed. They'll believe you when you say that it must be done right away.

If they agree to give you what you need, thank them and explain how it's going to help you. All of this may seem simple, but most advertising people respond best to sensitive and sympathetic handling. And most of the time they don't get it.

Although meetings with clients have the advantage of face-to-face contact, they usually involve significant travelling time between premises. With the constant exception of presenting creative work, the vast majority of client contact, and especially on unplanned immediate matters, can be done by phone. Let messengers and facsimile machines transfer paperwork to and fro. But meet clients from time to time, of course.

Thinking time

Accounts need to be thought about as well as handled. In fact, account handling work should include thinking. Yet it's so easy to slip into a reactive mould, and simply service the client.

Agency work can be very hectic and its constant intrusions can prevent deep thought. However, as most thought takes place in your subconscious, which has unlimited potential, your mind can help you even when you're working flat out.

The easiest way to deal with a problem, or work out how to realize an opportunity, is to 'sleep on it'. Given appropriate instruction, your mind can work through the night while you are asleep. And it doesn't even disturb you.

Like the agency's creative department, your mind needs a clear brief and time on its own, free from minute-to-minute interruption. Then it can solve problems.

Handling check

1   Do you know what you want to achieve each day?
2   Do you make a note of the things you know you want to achieve each day? (Or do you have a perfect memory with instant recall?)
3   Do you go out of your way to achieve your goals?
4   Do you know what you are already committed to doing next week?
5   Do you *sell* the agency effectively on the phone?
6   Do you know what you want to achieve on each call. (Do you normally achieve it?)
7   Do you encourage the client to speak his mind and do you allow enough time?
8   How do you think the client usually feels about the agency after speaking with you?
9   Do you keep your written work brief?
10 Do you get written work done efficiently through dictation or outside office hours?
11 Do you provide your clients with estimates of the cost of each production job? Are they accurate?
12 Do you invoice your clients promptly and explain any variation from estimate?
13 Do you deal efficiently with the paperwork you receive?
14 Do you get the urgent things done first?
15 Do you spend more time on the most important things? (And the least amount of time on the least important things?)

16 Do you help to ensure that meetings are properly prepared?
17 And do you help steer each meeting towards making decisions (wherever decisions need to be made)?
18 Do you allow yourself time to think?

Part II
Creating campaigns

Chapter 5

Getting into gear

Start by listening

Suppose that you start out facing a client who has one or many products, or corporate image, jobs or whatever, to sell. Each agency starts most assignments by taking an overview of the product to be sold, its problems and its opportunities. You need to learn what *has* been going on, and then take a preliminary view on the viability of the client's marketing objectives. Finally you'll consider what advertising could do to help.

Unfortunately, rules about how advertising should be used don't always carry well between markets or even different time periods. The known factors about how advertising has worked are often outweighed by the unknown. So usually you must consider the whole of the selling process, the product's own strengths and weaknesses, its consumers' tastes and how they are changing, as well as what the competition is up to and how it is likely to behave in the future. This is a major task.

Your client's ultimate objective is to make profits. He should be aware of how much profit his company can make from each extra sale and therefore how much it's worth spending to get these sales. If he has an idea of how many sales advertising is likely to create, he should be able to formulate an advertising budget. However, this is often determined before the agency becomes involved, which can be too late. And your client's estimated advertising budget may be too small to achieve the extra sales. Beware!

You'll probably assess what past advertising has been trying to achieve and how, and how well each campaign has worked. You may try to establish why each campaign succeeded or not, and use experience of other markets – and past experience in the same market – to assess the likely performance of your advertising.

You must form a view on what any given advertising budget is likely to achieve, and hence the size of budget needed to achieve the advertiser's targets. Your agency's experience might quite quickly lead you to think that the advertising could be more effective or that the client's product is in decline, or to almost any other conclusion. You may feel that the budget is too small, or quite realistic; agencies seldom feel that an advertising budget is too big!

You should develop a view on the purpose of the advertising and *how* it will help sales or develop image.

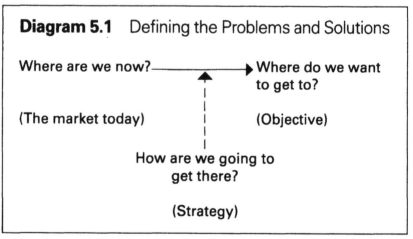

Diagram 5.1   Defining the Problems and Solutions

Where are we now?⸻⟶Where do we want
to get to?

(The market today)   (Objective)

How are we going to
get there?

(Strategy)

As you establish the advertising's *objective* through discussions, your agency will start trying to work out how it can be realized through a *strategy* or *sales argument*: the reason why a customer should buy your client's products rather than anyone else's. What is it that your advertiser alone is really *offering*?

This could be a feature of his product or service which really is distinct, or just a benefit that no-one else has yet made a song and dance about. You can cause people to look at the product in a different way and buy it for a new set of reasons, or you can create an emotional advantage for your product. In some markets, the products are so similar that the advertising is the only real difference. Arguably, it's an emotional benefit.

The strategy will in time provide the 'platform' for your advertising: a springboard for the creative team who are going to receive your brief.

What to ask clients to get good briefs

The best agencies work *with* their clients and use their knowledge. You should start your thinking where the client leaves off, using his thinking as a starting point for your own. Most clients won't set out to educate the agency about its task. You'll have to ask.

The onus is on you, to find out what the advertiser already knows. Always watch out for his pearls of wisdom, or the throwaway thought that brings the product to life. (He may use such words without recognizing their advertising strength.) So you start the briefing process with the advertiser.

You'll want to find out how his product is made, what goes into it, how it is developed, how it is sold. You may have to search high and low for things that differentiate it – or could be used to differentiate it – from the competition. You'll also be looking for stories that could be featured in the advertising. (Your client's salesmen are often a better goldmine for these than the brand or product manager.)

Potential advertising ideas are often triggered by closely examining the product. The more angles you look at it from, the more likely you are to discover a strong advertising message. Research can tell you more. You can discover clues about the customers' preferences through what was bought and what wasn't. With any luck your client already knows a great deal about how his products sell and under what conditions. He's got the benefit of experience, unless it's a new product. Learn what you can.

If he's been in business for some time but hasn't learnt all that he can from the past, you may have to become his historian, and go through all the files. What happened during the last advertising campaign? When did sales increase? And what caused the changes?

Of course, each product will have different strengths, and you may need to approach each one individually. Nevertheless, some questions are standard. And before you interrogate the product, you should interrogate the client: establish his ambitions.

Start with recent history. Sales data are vital and you probably want all that are available. You might discover that the 80:20 rule applies here, i.e. that 80 per cent of your client's sales come from 20 per cent of his customers. And you need a history of the client's promotional work, so that you can look for causes and effects. Then you can get straight into ambitions. What does he really *want* to do with the product or, if appropriate, his company? Where does he want it to be in, say, five years' time? Does he have a business plan? Business plans describe a company or product's strengths, competitive advantage and positioning together with projections for future income and costs. They're very useful to advertising agencies.

Costs

You'll probably want to understand your client's cost structure. How much does it cost him to make each product, and how much profit will he make from each extra sale?

You should ensure that there is no confusion between *average* costs (the total costs involved in making, say, a product line divided by the number actually made) and *marginal* costs (the cost of making one more unit). For example, a million chocolate bars might cost £100,000 to make (an average cost of 10 pence per bar) but making another 10,000 bars might cost £500 (a marginal cost of just 5 pence) if, for instance, there is surplus machine time available.

The same distinction applies to revenue. Your client might be able to sell a million bars to retailers at 12 pence per bar (yielding a profit of £120,000) but in order to *sell* another 10,000 he might have to drop the price of the goods by a penny to 11 pence. His marginal revenue would be less than his average revenue.

Find out your client's annual budgets and goals, and how he arrived at them. This information will always come in handy later when you're pitching for a bigger budget. If he's got a business plan, he's probably quantified his sales and made some assumptions about the customers he's planning to attract. If you have a good idea of what additional sales are worth to your client, you'll have more idea how much he ought to spend on advertising.

Customers

The person you really need to know most about, however, is the client's customer. The more you understand the customer, the better you can sell the product. It's surprising how much some companies know about their customers, and astounding how little other companies seem to have learnt.

Do you know why people are buying the product? Do you know who's making the decision, the husband or child, the wife or some combination? And do you know how they use your product? As an occasional alternative to the competition or as an essential? And do you know how they feel about your product? How would *they* describe it?

What does your client know about the total size of his market? And do you know what market your client is in? He might think that he's a major company playing in a small market while all along he's a smaller player in a very big market, most of which he's chosen to ignore. Once you know your client's sales goals and the likely future size of market, you're in a position to infer what percentage of the market he's aiming for. Is this realistic?

What is your own advertising budget supposed to be? How many sales per £1,000 expenditure are implied? How did your client's last campaign do, and how did this compare to his goals? Does your client normally achieve his goals or is he over-optimistic?

How much are the competition spending on their products, and with what result? Do you know why previous campaigns have been so successful/disappointing?

It's worth making sure that you get all these pieces of consumer information out of your client. They could be vital to your future advertising strategy.

A promise

You may also be able to learn from your client's past advertising strategy. What is the proposition that he's put to the consumer? Is your current brief to find a new strategy or to use the old one? Should you start your strategic thinking by evaluating that proposition and making a recommendation?

Yesterday's promise may be too bold, too weak or simply irrelevant. You may have to find out. At the very least, you must take a view.

Bearing in mind what you've learnt about the consumer, what do you know about the offer that you ought to be making? The biggest limitations on sales could be the advertising proposition, the product's packaging, its price, distribution, the quality of the product itself, or what the competition get up to. If you've got time, you had better consider them all.

Handling check

1   Can the client give a detailed picture of his sales? (How can they be broken down?)
2   What are his business objectives for the next year/five years?
3   Which product does he plan to sell more of?
4   How much is that business worth? (How much more? How profitable?)
5   What does he know about his customers?
6   What has he defined about the new customers he wants?
7   How many? (What's the size of the market? What market share is he aiming for?)
8   What does he think customers need from his kind of product? (What might they look for?)
9   What does he know about how they choose between products?
10   How long does it take them to choose?
11   What do they think of his product?
12   What sort of research has he done and what has he learnt?
13   What does he have to offer that's different? (What does he consider his unique selling proposition?)
14   Why aren't *potential* customers already choosing him (as much as he wants)?
15   How do you need to change customers' feelings about the product?
16   How? (e.g. speed or breadth of service, thoroughness, add-on services.)
17   What is the competition saying, how and where?
18   How can the advertising differentiate the product? (e.g. in what it says, by the tone it takes, where it says it.)
19   What has the client been doing? (In advertising as well as other promotion.)
20   How well has it worked? (Why?)

Sell what people buy

There are good reasons for today's obsession with marketing. Effective marketing separates tomorrow's winners from tomorrow's losers. But beware. The word has a number of dimensions.

'Marketing consultancies' are mostly agencies who work below-the-line and produce work which doesn't end up as advertising in editorial-carrying media. They offer every kind of promotional help. Usually, they don't get to do advertising, as advertising agencies work very hard to prevent them. Nevertheless, marketing is a useful word for the promotional agencies since it stakes a claim to a wide area of competence. 'Marketing departments' can have a broad responsibility for every promotional activity undertaken for their company. From the advertising agencies' point of view, marketing is an umbrella term which covers advertising as well as all that's in any way related.

Marketing also describes a way of thinking. In marketing parlance there are three kinds of company. Some are product-led. They take their existing product range as given and their engineers, scientists, or whoever, think up new ones from time to time. In sales-led companies there is a deliberate effort to maximize sales. For example, they might actively look for more retail outlets in order to do so. But they won't be marketing-led. So what does a marketing-led company do?

Its starting point is the customer. He's (or she's) always right. This kind of company doesn't have a long-term plan to sell any particular product. On the contrary, its goal is to sell what people want. That means adapting its sales and promotional plans accordingly. These may sound like small differences. But, believe me, the difference in state of mind between product-led companies and marketing-led companies is enormous.

Here's a litmus test. Suppose a company has two products. Product A exceeds sales targets, causing resource problems, and product B falls short of target. The product-led company will cut product A's promotional budget in order to solve the resource problem, and switch the funds to product B in order to help it reach the target. The marketing-led company will increase the expenditure on product A in order to exploit the market fully and take advantage of the lower cost of sales. And it will put its energies into solving product A's resource problem and deciding whether to develop product B, whose budget may be cut, or to drop it in favour of new product C!

So this product/sales/marketing split cuts deep. And it has big consequences. Today's marketing wisdom is that the marketing-led companies will triumph, all other things being equal. Success depends upon your reading of the market.

Go a little deeper

Your brand manager's view of his product is seldom the only one in the company you need. If you don't know the company, you might want to explore its staff's attitudes in some depth. You might try interviewing them in the following kind of way. (If you don't know your client's answers to these questions, you may be short of useful knowledge.)

1. How long have you been with the company?
2. What job do you do now? (Why did you choose it?)
3. And what were you doing previously? (At the company and elsewhere.)
4. What would you say were the strengths and weaknesses of your company?)
5. Which are your strongest competitors? (Why do you mention them?)
6. What are your company's biggest opportunities?
7. What are the things that give you the most satisfaction at work, and what are the things you would most like to change?
8. If the company were, say, a shop, (or a car or an animal) which one would it be most like?
9. Which advertising campaigns interest you? (Which do you like? Why?)

The answers can give you an insight into what is going on at the client's company and how the company sees itself and its products. This will help you to establish individual corporate ambitions.

Above all, you might develop an independent agency point of view on your client's marketing objectives. Can he really achieve what he's setting out to do? Has he a blinkered or over-rosy view of his product? Does he cling to some aspect of his product that consumers find irrelevant? Can he build sales *that* quickly? How much does the brand need to be built to achieve that level of sales? Does he have the necessary marketing resource: the budget? Is he being under-ambitious? Is there a more lucrative market need which his service could fulfil?

Fundamentals, like his product's positioning (how it is seen by the potential customers), may turn out to be wrong: he may be aiming at the wrong market; this could be researched. (Researching potential customers is almost always useful, if it can be afforded.)

As an account handler, you have to decide how much to get involved in all of these issues. Which are the ones that can be dealt with quickly? Where can you rely on your client's judgement? And which have to be thrashed all the way through?

Fortunately a good deal of basic fact-finding can usually be done quite quickly and cheaply. Information on advertising expenditure can be gained from Media Expenditure Analysis Limited (known as MEAL), together with a breakdown of where it is spent. Consumer spending data (usually 'Nielsen' reports) can be easily and quickly gathered. Competitive products can be assessed. So can their promotional material, from advertising to leaflets.

For consumer-type products, you may need to go further and test them amongst (potential) customers, especially if the client has not done so. After all, the consumers' view of your product is crucial to its success, and it *is* impartial. It is the reality you will have to work with.

Where the advertising brief concerns something less tangible, say a company's awareness and rating against its competitors, then a telephone research programme amongst a relatively large number of relevant people might be appropriate.

Handling check

1 What do you still need to learn?
2 What can the advertising industry's material tell you?
3 What can you learn from the competition (visiting their stores/ premises, reading their advertisements and literature, using their product etc.)?
4 Are there any relevant industry sources (e.g. trade associations) or useful public bodies or government departments?
5 Can the media department help?
6 What sort of press do the products get? (What do the journalists think?)
7 What do you know about what customers think of the products?
8 Will talking to some prospective customers give enough clues for now?

9   Do you need professional research help from outside the agency?

10 Can you afford it? (Who'll pay?)

11 Can you afford to be without it? (Should you risk spending a much larger amount of money on inappropriate advertising?)

12 *Exactly* what do you need to know?

13 And how reliable must the results be? (What level of confidence is needed and what margin for error can be allowed?)

14 So do we need qualitative research (usually in-depth with small numbers to explore feelings) or quantitative research (usually large numbers of people to explore facts)?

15 Will talking to some prospective customers give enough clues for now?

16 Who else in the client's organization could help (e.g. the salesmen) or elsewhere (e.g. journalists, stockbrokers' sector analysts)?

17 What is the agency's point of view?

Developing the product

Market research sometimes leads to unexpected conclusions. One possible finding is that your client's product needs to change. The product may not be capable of fulfilling the customer needs you have identified and you might see a bigger market share for a (slightly) different product.

Sometimes you can think this through yourself. Try taking a step away from your client's product and asking why it doesn't have twice its current level of sales. What are the barriers to much greater success? Would a bigger advertising expenditure get you there? (Perhaps it really ought to be doubled.) Or would the product need to include some different ingredients? Would it sell much more if it were cheaper? What could better packaging contribute? How does the product's name compare with its competition? What is its design communicating about the product?

Try making a list of all the needs your client's product is currently fulfilling. If you were trying to fulfil most of them, what would you call your product, how would you package it and how would you sell it? You might be surprised by your answers.

Handling check

1 Who is the product good for?
2 How big should its market share be? (Bigger than it currently is? Smaller than it currently is?)
3 Is it in the right market? Should it be competing against something else?
4 How could the product be modified?
5 Is its name right? (What would the best name be?)
6 Are the price, distribution and packaging appropriate?
7 If you started with the needs this product is trying to fulfil, what kind of product would you come up with?

Chapter 6

The big media decision

Media decisions are of two types: intermedia and intramedia. Intermedia decisions concern which kind(s) of media should be used in the campaign, e.g. television and posters, or press and radio. Intramedia decisions concern which medium should be used from within a particular kind of media, e.g. London Weekend Television or Central Television and Grampian.

The intermedia decision is usually made fairly early on in the advertising process, i.e. before the creative work is produced. The intramedia decisions are usually made when the creative work is complete, or nearly so. This may be quite frustrating. You involve your media planner or buyer at the outset, then you let him be while you switch to creative work, then you involve him once the creative work's mostly done, to fine-tune your planning and buy your media.

This chapter is concerned exclusively with the intermedia decision – or the big media decision, as I have called it.

How to brief your media department

You'll need to work with your media colleagues. As explained in Chapter 2, the media departments of most big agencies are made up of media planners and media buyers. The media planners decide which media to use, while media buyers buy time or space in planned media. Most big agencies have specialists who do nothing except buy time on television and commercial radio. At the other extreme, in the smaller agencies account handlers do their own media planning and buying.

Some advertisers choose to use an agency to create their advertising, and another organization to place it. This could be a full service advertising agency, since some of them are renowned for their media buying skills, or it could be a firm offering only media services known as a media independent.

However, account handlers usually work with their in-house creative and media departments simultaneously. And if you don't know which kind of media you are going to run in, you'll have to talk to media first. In practice, the two disciplines overlap. Good media planning usually means allowing media buyers to respond to buying opportunities as they crop up.

You'll probably thrash out some of the major media issues with your media colleagues, the account planner and probably someone from the creative department. But if you want the best results from your media department, your best plan is usually to do a proper brief. This doesn't have to cover all the same ground as the creative brief, but it does need to cover a lot of areas that do not concern the creative people. You're dealing with two quite distinct groups of people with their own crafts and their own concerns. Give your media department a tailor-made brief. It ought to cover the following areas:

1 Product objectives

What is your client's product and what is he trying to do with it? How ambitious is he now and in the future? What are his business goals, his sales targets and so on?

2 Advertising objectives

What is the role of advertising? What exactly is it supposed to be doing? Whether you are aiming to get people to try a product or to increase their brand loyalty imply different sorts of media solutions.

3   The competition

What do you already know about what the competition are doing, how and where they advertise, and how successful they're being? You might end up wanting to avoid them by advertising elsewhere. Your media department need to know where the competition is.

4   Media objectives

Must the advertising reach a particular percentage of your target audience, or can the campaign be focused upon a segment of the audience? How many times must the audience be exposed to the advertising? You might feel that you'll need to get your message home at least half a dozen times before it begins to work. What do you have in mind about the sort of length of the commercial or the size of press advertisement?

5   Budget

If a budget has been set, you had better tell the media department what it is. You'll need to make clear whether or not it includes VAT, advertising agency commission and production costs. Misunderstandings here could put your spending plan out by up to 50 per cent or more.

6   Target audience

Everything you know about the target audience ought to go in here. It's seldom enough. Try to provide an in-depth portrait. What kind of people are they? Innovative media solutions tend to come from in-depth briefings.

7   Regionality

In Britain, television is bought nationally or regionally, radio is bought locally, the national press has a southern bias and posters are mostly in towns. Where is your client's product bought most?

Where are the heaviest users and where are the light users? How does this relate to the advertising objectives and audience definition? Is the client after heavy users or light users?

8 Seasonality

Are there periods of peak consumption and relative lows? If they are predictable, tell your media department. It will probably affect the plan. Television is cheapest in January because demand for airtime is at its lowest.

9 Campaign timing

The timing of the campaign may be fixed. It may be for a limited period or open-ended, success-related or set in stone. Tell them about the timing and what this depends on.

10 Creative considerations

What impact is any possibly favoured kind of creative treatment likely to have on media planning? If it is, for example, the agency's feeling that this brand needs the life and warmth of television, tell them now, not later.

Handling check

1 What, exactly, is the product/service?
2 Who do you want to reach? (The 'target audience' for the advertising.) What kind of people are they? How many of them must be exposed to the advertising?
3 What objectives must the media solution achieve?
4 Are regional and seasonal consumption figures relevant?
5 What does the audience think of the product?
6 What percentage of the total relevant audience must be exposed to the advertising?
7 How many times, on average, must they be exposed to the message (often called 'opportunities to see', or 'OTS')?
8 And how soon after they see it the first time should they see it again and so on (frequency)?

9   What type of media does the advertising task lend itself to? (Has the kind of media already been decided?)
10   What does the creative strategy imply about the choice of media (e.g. forceful, dominant, newsworthy or having a long life)?
11   Must the audience be continually reminded through advertising repeatedly?
12   For television and radio, how long must the airtime be (30 seconds, 40 seconds etc.) or how big must the advertisements be (e.g. whole page, double page spread) or can the media specialist take a view on these issues?
13   When must the advertising campaign break?
14   And when must it finish?
15   Has the client already talked with any media? (If so, who, and what has been agreed?)
16   When is the media work needed?

Fortunately, as an account handler you don't have to be a media expert. You just have to know how to get the best out of your media department.

Media pros and cons

Having an insight into the possible value of each potential medium will help you. What follows is a brief discussion of some media characteristics you should keep in mind.

1   The small screen

Television is the most intensive medium. Most of the largest national advertisers spend most of their advertising money on television. It reaches virtually the whole population, which cannot be said of any other medium. However, it costs a great deal to buy audiences through television, both in the cost of buying airtime, in which each commercial has a 'spot', and through the production costs of making a television commercial.

In creative terms, it's the ideal medium for bringing a brand to life, as it offers sound, colour and movement. However, it's difficult to get across a complicated message on television or communicate more than two or three facts in each commercial. This matters less often than you might think: advertising usually has to be simple if it is to work. And although your client might want to say a lot about his product, in most cases the consumer doesn't want to know, as the product constitutes only the smallest part of his or her life. Moreover, the consumer probably doesn't need the advertising to tell him much in order to be sold on the product, providing it's a reasonable one.

Alternatively, you can use television to build a brand's positioning in the minds of your customers while another advertising medium, say the press, communicates the support information.

Suppose you've chosen television, you've still got to decide how long your commercial(s) should be. You can buy 10, 20, 30, 40, 50 or 60-second slots, or longer. Your media department may have an in-built bias towards shorter commercials, in order to maximize audience coverage and frequency of message, while your creative team will almost certainly want a long commercial in order to develop their central message.

A 60-second slot allows you time to create a mood, which is more difficult in a 30-second slot. Does your client *need* to create a mood, or will the basic proposition be enough? Anything shorter is simply a one-point message which usually acts only as a reminder. There's just enough time to register your brand name and promise, but not enough time to *persuade*.

Your campaign doesn't have to consist of only one single-length commercial. You might, for instance, start the campaign with 60-second slots to get the brand's personality across, switch to 30-seconds until the proposition is firmly established and finally go to 10-second reminders – all with one commercial. If you are going to do this sort of thing, you have to shoot your commercial with three different finished lengths in mind – two cut-down versions of one long commercial. The longer your commercials, the less of your audience you cover or the lower the frequency with which you reach them or both.

Television's coverage of your target audience is measured in percentages, called television rating points, or TVRs for short. So a schedule which brought you a 25 per cent coverage of your market would be said to have 25 TVRs. And, of course, coverage can itself be traded for frequency. You have to decide how thinly the message can be spread.

2 *Press*

Newspapers are almost as big a medium as television. In some countries more is spent on the press than on television. In Britain, the newspaper industry is booming mainly through the use of new technology; indeed, in the 1980s more titles have been launched than have folded.

The press allows you a lot more flexibility to choose between audiences. You can probably reach more of the audiences you want, with less wastage than on television. And you can communicate a great deal of information about your product, or use a great deal of copy to persuade. You can 'talk' for much longer than is possible on television. And you have the *chance* to hold your audiences' attention for much longer per penny spent. Moreover, the press is more permanent than television. Readers can go back to your advertisement again and again while they are thinking about buying your product.

It's flexible in another way too. You can choose the context in which you want your advertisement to appear more exactly than on television. What editorial environment would best suit your product? However, you'll usually have to pay for the privilege of specifying where you want to be in the paper. Buying 'run of paper' i.e. a space which is situated anywhere in the paper at the media owner's discretion, is cheaper. You may have to pay a special premium to appear in a particular section, e.g. the women's pages, or simply to choose a particular page.

And you can choose what size of press advertisement to have. What size should you choose? Certain rules usually apply. The bigger your *message*, the bigger the space you'll need. A major thought or claim squeezed into a small space tends to lack credibility. A long message needs a big space too. The more you need to *reassure* the customer about your product, the bigger the space you'll need. A big space also makes the client look like a major company. A small one, of course, will make him look small. If you want to be a brand leader, you've got to look like one.

So the press can make your client look big relatively cheaply. On the downside, however, it can't show his product in colour, except in a small, but increasing, number of newspapers. And it can't bring his product to life through sound or movement, which makes product demonstrations difficult.

Of course, newspapers also take a lot of small advertisements which require no account handling at all. A significant proportion of their advertising revenue comes from classified advertising.

3   Magazines

Magazines have a longer life than newspapers. They offer high quality colour, making them better at communicating your client's brand image. You can use them to reach specific groups of people such as teenagers, sport enthusiasts or investors. And their editorial environment can reflect favourably upon your product. Specialist products can gain from the authority of nearby specialist editorial.

It's a reflection of magazines' success as an advertising medium that many of them are bulging with advertisements, probably including your client's competition. Your ideal is to be the only advertiser who is reaching your customers through a particular medium. The prevalence of other magazine advertisers is likely to dilute your client's message.

Many magazines are read by more than one person, and many magazine readers look at the advertising. Some of them will wade through pages of it rather than skip to the editorial. Indeed, they value their magazines partly for their advertising. There are probably two reasons for this. Most of a magazine's advertisements are relevant to its readers. And most magazine advertising is pleasant to look at.

4   Posters

Your art director is likely to be keen on posters. They give him the chance to put a simple message in a big space. They are either side of urban streets on wooden hoardings, and they move through streets on buses and taxis as well as inside them. And they're visible at railway stations, airports and bus shelters, as you get on to and off transport.

Your media department can buy sites throughout Britain, in one urban centre or outside just one supermarket to remind shoppers of your campaign's promise. I once ran a campaign in the colour press with the addition of just one poster site: outside the client's headquarters. You can be that choosy.

Posters are bought in 'sheet' sizes, generally as 4-sheet, 16-sheet and 48-sheet sizes. 48-sheet is just over 3 metres tall by 6 metres wide. They're usually bought for a month at a time. It's cheaper to buy a package than to specify individual sites.

There's a limit to what you can say on an outdoor poster. You've got to shout fast, and complete your message in seconds. Indoor posters are different. Tube, taxi and bus riders have minutes available to read your message, if it interests them. And tube and bus riders tend to repeat their journey again and again, exposing themselves to your message over and over.

Posters have enormous impact and can dominate their environment. They're very intrusive, but they don't offer sound or movement.

5   *Cinemas*

Cinema advertising does. And once you're in the cinema the big screen is the most intrusive medium of all. It's also the least restrictive from a creative point of view, and offers better sound and picture quality than television.

It's expensive to make films for cinemas but quite cheap to buy the spots. You can buy nationally or regionally, or you can go right down to one cinema, as many local advertisers do.

But cinemas offer your client a very incomplete audience. The biggest audience is 15–24 year-olds, and 35-and-overs cannot be reached in large numbers.

6   *Radio*

Radio offers sound, and that's all it takes to sell many products. It's cheap both in terms of airtime and the cost of producing the commercial. And it can be bought and produced quickly. Moreover, it's possible to reach people through radio not long before they make their day's major purchase or do their shopping. The memory of a television commercial usually fades overnight.

Although commercial radio stations are local in their individual coverage, it is possible to use a lot of them to build a national campaign. And while each spot may be listened to by only a few people, low costs mean that it is possible to build coverage over time by repeating your commercial. However, this also means that some people will be exposed to your client's commercial a lot, and they may get sick of it.

As radio lacks a visual image, you have to use your radio commercial's sounds to conjure your product up in the listener's mind. You should try to stretch his imagination. It's even more difficult to communicate detailed information on radio than it is on television. But you can point listeners to the rest of your campaign or invite them to call up.

The biggest limitation for some advertisers is the audience that commercial radio tends to attract. With the exception of the Capital/LBC airplay in London, there is no more than one station per area. So your only way of choosing your kind of audience is to try and buy time around the kinds of programme which your audience is likely to listen to. As luck would have it, account handlers don't have to make the choice alone.

Chapter 7

Putting the brief in

Some account handlers don't know a creative brief from a 999 call. Yet a good brief is as much as 50 per cent of your advertising problem solved.

It's the foundation stone on which the creative and media work is built, because it defines the advertising task and allows your agency to start working towards an objective. At its simplest, the brief explains what needs to be said so that the creative people can decide *how* to say it. I know a copywriter who insists that all briefs can be boiled down to 'WHO IS SAYING WHAT, TO WHOM?', where the who is the advertiser, the what is the strategy or proposition, and the whom is the target audience. (And the only possible addition is 'WHAT'S GOOD ABOUT *THAT*?')

You may have worked through volumes of information about your client's product, but the finished advertising can only communicate so much (probably only one idea and some supporting material). The advertising brief's goal is to achieve a clarity of thought and express it in its most concise form. However, too many account handlers skimp on briefs. They simply pass on the information that has come their way. This can create great frustration, as the following note which was found in a leading UK agency shows.

Announcing a new briefing system for our Agency

The old system, using yellow sheets with summaries of strategies and objectives etc., is obviously not producing the advertisements our clients require.

So here's the new system.

First, make a list of all the facts about the client's product or service.

Second, make a list of all the points the client thinks are important (include any suggested headlines, slogans, baselines, etc).

Get your secretary to type each separate fact/ suggestion, leaving plenty of space between each one.

Ask her to get a pair of scissors, and cut each fact/ suggestion out separately.

Now put all these separate pieces of paper into a hat. Shake the hat about a bit. Then pull out, say, six pieces of paper. These pieces of paper are the brief.

I'm convinced this system will work much more effectively than the old yellow sheets.

This bitter memorandum must have been written by a creative person, as they have nothing but your brief and their own commonsense to work from. It outlines a common advertising problem.

Some poor account handlers simply collect every piece of information they can find and dump it on a creative desk. Research, reports, old advertisements, competitive advertisements, companies' annual reports, more old advertisements, a copy of every publication on the media schedule, anything. I know of one agency desk where there's a 3 inch high model of a railway workman from a train set. The anonymous figure is carrying a large sack of coal on his back. Under the model, our writer has affixed the caption, 'I've brought the brief, where shall I put it?'

As an aid to a good brief, with a single clear distilled piece of thinking attached to it, all relevant information can be helpful. But in the absence of a clear direction to go in, a mass of information is useless. How are the creative people to know what is relevant and what isn't? How much time will they waste simply reading it? How much more time understanding it?

A better brief

A writer still talks about the *best* brief he ever received. It was for a leather company. This firm supplied leather to the shoe trade, the clothing trade, the furniture trade, etc. The briefing material ran to 23 pages. On the first page was the brief, which went something like: In no one particular aspect of the 5 things which matter most to our target market is our client stunningly exceptional. However, the slight superiority he demonstrates in each of these areas of importance adds up to a *very* much better company than anyone else in his field. The areas are: quality control, delivery dates, pricing, the ability to innovate, responsiveness to customer needs. Please produce one colour double-page spread for each of these topics.

There followed 22 closely-typed pages, collected by the company over a period of months, of hundreds of actual examples that demonstrated the very five points the agency thought should be made. There was also a factory visit for the creative team, a verbal debriefing and discussion about target markets, plus other relevant information.

But the beauty of the brief was its single-mindedness. 'Here's what will convince the target market. Here are examples you can use. Pick the ones that will translate into simple, memorable, convincing advertisements.'

Of course, some products are easy to understand: a can of lager, a soap, food. Here, your creative team will have no difficulty with the product itself. But your product's positioning in the minds of its customers will have to be *very* clearly defined. Your target market's attitudes are vital. (A 22-year-old creative team may find it difficult to empathize with the needs and aspirations of a 45-year old C2 housewife.) Slight competitive product differences may become the crux of the brief. The aim is to make your brief point clearly to the most valuable area of creative thinking, so that your team doesn't waste time on irrelevant solutions.

If you have an almost incomprehensible product (and some products are – the outer edges of hi-fi, construction industry products, specialist financial areas, new developments in information technology) – you are out of luck. You will simply have to do a lot of homework. First, it will take you a lot of time simply to understand the product, and then to understand what's good about it. Then you must understand what benefit this gives to the target market. It might even be difficult to understand the target audience itself.

Writing a brief for difficult, obscure or specialist products and services is tough because at the end of all your understanding, you've still got to translate it into a simple, clear advertising brief: 'This is what our client's offering, here's what our target audience wants to know about it, and this is what will prove the point.' You are aiming for simplicity.

It's worth all the hard work, though. A good creative team will be grateful for your clear insight. It makes their job much easier, and means they'll probably work much harder for you. Then you're on to a winner.

Even on difficult products, you must not duck the issues. Waffle will not help you. And if it isn't discovered sooner, your poor brief would probably be found out once the creative work is produced and turns out substandard or off-strategy. Consider the following story.

Once, there was a world-beating process which resulted in super-light structures for thousands of end-products, from airplane galleys and wings to a new generation of lightweight skis. (The account handler only knew these two.) Don't do what that account handler did: he stood in front of the creative team with a 3 inch lump of airplane galley in one hand and a 3 inch lump of lightweigh ski in the other, saying 'But *here* is your product . . . and *here* is your product. I do not understand your difficulty.' The creative team re-wrote his brief, substituting the word 'eggs' for the product and 'Martians' for the target market. It didn't help, but it made them feel better. Then they went to the client for a real brief.

Good briefs can lead to good work, better briefs to better work, and a misleading brief to misleading work. It's as simple as that. 'Garbage in, garbage out' means that if a bad brief goes into your creative department, bad work will emerge. A good brief will get *used*. It may well get thumbprints on it and coffee spilt over it as the creative team constantly refer to it to check any relevant idea.

A good brief also helps the creative team get work approved by the agency's creative director. He can quickly see whether the brief has been answered. And it helps busy advertising agency managing directors and chairmen to judge an advertisement; at least the brief tells them what the advertising is *supposed* to be saying about the product.

When it comes to briefing, some account handlers have help from the account planners. The extent to which they are used is partly at the discretion of the account handlers. Some agencies have lots of account planners, others have very few, or even none. While some advertising tasks require lots of 'planning', others are absolutely straightforward. Even when an account planner is present to lighten your load, the account handler takes responsibility for the brief.

The brief sets in stone what the advertising ought to achieve and what the creative team must apply their minds to. So it's the yardstick by which their work will be judged: 'Is the creative work on strategy?' How can you be sure that your brief is up to scratch?

As well as the strategic choice, your brief must cover all important details. Like exactly what is needed: ideas on concept boards or storyboards, when the work must be completed, with truthful deadlines! Also your client's company name, its product name and corporate house rules (for example on typefaces and logos); which media the advertising will run in and what size/length the finished advertising will be; any production budget restrictions.

Most companies have a positioning statement on themselves or the brand or both, which the agency may have helped develop. This is simply a definition of what the consumers are supposed to think about it, e.g. 'an efficient company to work with' or 'a refreshing product'. This needs to accompany the brief as well.

What's in a brief?

A number of descriptions are needed, apart from defining the advertiser and the thing to be advertised.

1   The work you require

The creative work can range from campaign ideas to complete scripts for a 60-second commercial, from headlines for a press campaign to revisions to last year's copy. The *job* has to be specified. If you don't say exactly what you want, you probably won't get it.

2   The audience

This defines who the advertiser is trying to reach and is normally called the 'target audience'. He could be aiming the advertising at lightweight consumers of his own brand, or heavy users of a competing brand, or even of a different kind of product. Knowing who are being aimed at, and their current relationship to the product, is vital.

The audience may have describable characteristics. Their age, sex, wealth, class, values and lifestyle are likely to be relevant to the advertising task. If so, they should be included.

3   The objective

Advertising objectives can vary widely from creating a *particular* feeling about the brand, a 'positioning' in the minds of the consumers, to getting new customers to try the product, perhaps to lift it off the shelf when they are next in the supermarket. Or to send money.

'To sell more goods' simply won't do. (I've never come across an agency whose objective was to help clients sell fewer products.) Nor is 'To produce an A4-sized leaflet' an objective. Nor is 'To maximize coupon response'. (Your team might produce an advertisement that would produce thousands of coupons, all of them irrelevant, in which case your client would not thank you.)

It can be tempting to define the task broadly, and to ask the advertising to reach all relevant audiences with a multi-purpose message. Of course, a *campaign* consisting of a number of advertisements can help achieve a number of things. But advertising campaigns usually work best when they try to achieve just one thing, and successfully communicate one message to one audience. Then the advertising is single-minded. Having understood the product's potential and assessed alternative advertising strategies, you commit to paper the *single* most important advertising task. That is the objective.

4   The strategy

The advertising strategy is the message that is going to get you to your objective. It defines the product's 'selling proposition' or 'key thing' which can be used in order to achieve the objective. A soap bar could be described as 'fresh', a new mortgage product as 'a better way to buy your home'. It may also need a 'support' or proof.

Stated simply, a proposition is the idea that sells. It will be reflected in how the product is seen and might be described in anything from a colourful and slightly complicated proposition to just one word, e.g. 'refreshment'. Even though you might want to write a book about what the product can do, the strategy should not be longer than a sentence or two.

5   The guidelines

This is a 'miscellaneous' category covering any constraints upon the advertising. For example, the tone of the advertising may be pre-determined, humour *may* be prohibited or required, the advertising's typeface may be prescribed, and so on. Budget, length of commercial/size of advertisement, and chosen media usually fall into this last category.

Of course, you should add supporting facts which either help prove the proposition or just might help the creative team. You must give them guidelines to work within. If the team aren't aware of any particular constraint upon their work, from budget to style, they're likely to ignore it and produce irrelevant, if imaginative, work. Tone, imagery and colour constraints are important to the brief.

6   Timing

The time you allow for creative and media people to do their work and see it through to its appearance can be critical. Usually, the more time you allow, the better the work. *Creating* advertising involves many stages. For example, on a press advertisement you should allow time for the recipients of your brief to:

i)   Receive the brief
ii)   Understand the product
iii)   Come up with the concept
iv)   Get internal approval

v)   Get client approval
vi)   Get a budget approved
vii)   Write the advertising copy
viii) Get internal approval
ix)   Get client approval
x)   Get a picture taken/drawn
xi)   Get internal approval
xii)   Get client approval
xiii) Put the advertisement together
xiv)   Get internal approval
xv)   Get client approval
xvi)   Get proofs made
xvii) Get proofs signed
xviii) Meet media copy dates

The more complicated your product, the longer you should allow for stages (ii), (iii), and (vii), (x) and (xiii). Remember, too, that your creative team may also be working on five other concepts, re-doing two more, and putting another couple of advertisements together.

Once you've taken a view on all these matters you should be able to complete the briefing form. One more thing. You should cut your brief down wherever possible. It's easy to obscure a good thought with redundant waffle. A good creative brief is brief.

Handling check

1 What is the firm's name? (The client)
2 What are they selling? (Product/service)
3 What is the name of this project? (Campaign)
4 What does the agency need to produce? (Requirement – concepts and copy? Storyboard?)
5 To whom is the client selling? (The target audience)
6 What do you want to achieve for the advertiser? (The advertising objective)
7 What do you want the audience to think about the product? (Strategy)
8 What is the product's key advantage?
9 What rules must be followed in producing the advertising? (Guidelines)
10 In what media will it appear? (What size advertisement/length

CREATIVE BRIEF				
Client Campaign		Product Requirement		
Target audience				
Objective				
Strategy				
Guidelines				
Media	Date	BW/Col	Size	Copy dates
Author		date		work due
Team copy		art		traffic
Approvals	MD	AD	PD	CD

of commercial? Full colour or black and white or black plus one colour? Where in a publication? When on television?)

11 How much can be spent on making the advertisement? (The production budget)
12 When is the initial creative work needed for internal review? (The internal review date)
13 Does this information fit on one page?
14 Have you also supplied copies of any relevant past advertisements, competitors' campaigns and product brochures?

How to get your brief approved

In most agencies, you can't simply write an advertising brief and give it to a creative team. Some of your colleagues must also approve the brief.

One or more of your account directors, board director in charge and agency managing director will be involved in signing off the brief, so you've got an opportunity to learn from their judgement. Their particular strength should be their understanding of the client. They should have a good idea of what kind of work your brief is likely to produce and what kind of work the client will buy. They may have good grounds for turning your brief down.

If you have a planning director, he's likely to have to approve it too. A planner may have helped to write it. He's likely to be especially clever – planners usually are – and so he might be able to spot a weakness that you've missed.

Your creative director may have to approve the brief. He's likely to look at it from his department's point of view. Is it likely to lead to good work? Is it comprehensible? Is a reasonable amount of time allowed to do the work? Is all the information there?

Depending on how your agency is structured, you might go and see these people individually or you might simply give your brief to your traffic department for them to get approval or comments.

Your traffic department will have their own perspectives. They're concerned with workload and timing. Does the creative team who are assigned to this account have enough available time to do the job in the time you've allocated, or do they have too much else on? (They're probably busy.) Have you left enough time between the review date and the advertising's scheduled media appearances to get the advertisement approved and made? What is your contingency if the creative team don't come up with the right idea or your client turns the work down? Have you specified a production budget?

If you've got the agency's traffic department on your side, you're probably home and dry.

Chapter 8

How to help your creative team

Working with the team

Many account handlers do not enjoy the respect of the creative teams they work with. One way round this is to make sure you discuss each advertising task with the creative team assigned to the task.

Most creative teams consist of just one art director, who is primarily responsible for the visual side of the advertising, and a copywriter who is primarily responsible for its verbal content. You must be sure that they understand and agree with the brief. It's no good simply supplying a written brief without discussing it.

The chosen strategy can be executed by the creative team anywhere within the creative box overleaf. Your creative people are looking for a solution that is within the limitations shown in the box. If you have any instincts about the final creative solution that go beyond the brief, you should throw them in at this stage. You will also need to show your team the advertising produced by other companies in this market.

Your team probably need to visit the advertiser's premises, and to become familiar with the product itself. Members of the different departments need to understand the particular product's (potential) customers.

Creatives should share the customers' point of view and the

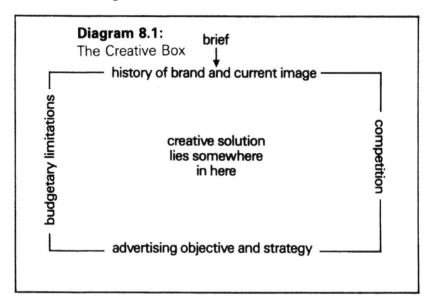

Diagram 8.1: The Creative Box

advertiser's aspirations. They'll bring plenty of healthy scepticism to bear on any advertiser's claims for his product. The creative team must *understand* what the prospective customers currently think of and feel about the brand and product, as well as what the advertiser wants them to think, if they are to bridge the gap between the current reality and the advertiser's objectives. Creatives should also *believe* in the product and the possibility of achieving the advertising task. You have to sell it to them on both counts, and inspire them with enthusiasm. You must communicate the product's virtues to the creative team so that they, in turn, can talk the customer round. If they can't be persuaded, there is probably something wrong with the brief. In fact, discussions with creatives are your last opportunity to spot a duff advertising brief.

Occasionally you may come across clients who want your agency to overclaim on their behalf. If you don't spot the overclaiming when you write the brief, you'll kick yourself when your creative team pulls it to shreds.

Handling check

1   Have you discussed the brief with the creative team?
2   And heard their point of view?
3   And provided them with a sense of purpose?
4   Do they understand the product and its markets?

5 And what the viewer/reader currently thinks of the product?
6 Have they got any ideas for the campaign?
7 Do they think you are interested in the product?
8 And excited by it?
9 Are they going in the right direction?
10 Are they motivated to give of their best?

Are they making progress?

Once your team set to work you should keep an eye on their progress. You shouldn't assume that the work will be ready on time, or it often won't be. However, if you have a reasonable creative team, you don't want to get in their hair by bothering them too much.

They are likely to be working for other account handlers too. Some of their jobs may have been labelled 'extremely urgent', in which case your task is likely to get pushed down their work list. You may need to keep it near the top. If you get into timing difficulties you might alert others to your problem – either your traffic department or your account director may be able to help.

Although you may have clearly explained the advertising task and even though your team feel they know what to do, there may be something that they still haven't understood about the product, its markets or its audience. If you have a discussion or two you may find out what it is.

How will your creative team start work on your assignment? First, they are going to read your brief and listen to your briefing.

Secondly, if you've allowed them enough time to do the work, they'll study all the facts that could influence the solution. They're better off learning at the beginning than when they think they *might* have a solution.

Thirdly, they'll confirm in their own minds whether your brief makes sense. It's at this point that they might come back to you with a problem on your brief – not enough facts, or some facts that don't fit. If they are still going forward at this point, they'll very probably deliver work that's at least satisfactory.

Fourthly, and most important, if they're good, they'll start to free-associate and make a note of every solution they can think up, however odd it appears to be! They won't settle for the first plausible solution that springs to mind. At this stage they won't use judgement to filter out apparently bad ideas. If you wander into their offices at this stage and ask them how they're doing, they probably won't know. That's why they'll probably say something like 'We've got some interesting ideas'.

Fifthly, they'll think of the ideal they're trying to achieve. What is it? What would the ideal look like? Then they'll start working through their ideas to see which measure up.

Sixthly, they'll start to use their judgement in working out which concept communicates most originally and clearly, and which useful techniques they've come up with.

You will need to monitor their progress week by week, and maintain day-to-day contact. Be friendly and sensitive. If they are in difficulty you probably need to sit down with them and talk it through. And start by listening.

The big problem is usually time. It can arise in two ways. You might only have allowed two weeks for your creative team to work on a campaign when six weeks would have done the job. Either the creative process gets cut to only a few hours for each of the stages we've just described, or worse, they omit some stages altogether. The creative stage of free association is often amongst the first to go. Or they get beaten by the clock and simply don't have any concept when you need one.

It's the mark of some good teams, and some bad ones, that they get beaten by the clock – your clock. Allow enough time. How much is enough? As much as you can get.

Even if you have allowed enough time for your creative team to tackle an assignment, the odds are that other account handlers have not. That's when you need to watch out. Your team might be tempted or pressured into doing the urgent work first at the expense of your work. In which case, they might only use the last two weeks of the six weeks you gave them to produce your campaign. In that case, why did you give them six weeks? You might as well have given them two, like everyone else. If this happens, make a fuss. Get your senior colleagues on the record that this is an exception which they won't let happen again. Then if it does, as it probably will, enlist their help. If this tactic fails, and it matters to you, it may be you're not working at the right agency.

If you've worked with the creative team before, you should have a good idea of their strengths and weaknesses and be able to sense whether they are making progress and when they are running into difficulties. You should know their standards, and be able to predict whether you will be happy with their work. If you know what kind of thing to expect, you won't be let down.

Handling check

1 Is your creative team attending to your task?
2 And making sufficient progress?
3 What is the main thing (if any) they still don't understand to their satisfaction?
4 How can you explain it?
5 Have your creative team got enough time to attend to your work?

Chapter 9

What's the big idea?

Reviewing creative work can be the most difficult job in advertising. It also requires sensitivity. At most agencies, junior account handlers aren't expected to express an opinion on creative work, but account directors invariably do.

Imagine that you are looking at some Pentel scribbles on a sheet of paper, perhaps mounted on a board. Or at a series of rough drawings for a commercial, a script idea, or a few sentences of copy. Not much to look at perhaps, but yours to judge. How should you set about judging it? You should probably keep any instinctive judgement to yourself for some time. And see how it settles. Instead, ask yourself some basic questions about the work. Is it on strategy? Does it communicate the benefit you set out to put across? Will it get attention? And does it reinforce the product's positioning?

It's a good ploy to discuss the concept or storyboard's strengths and weaknesses with the creative team who produced it (as tactfully, of course, as you can) to make sure you understand it. And you ought to try to see the work from the creative team's point of view. After all, they've been trying to see things from the customer's point of view. They may have succeeded.

Start by exploring their thinking and how they feel about the work they've done. Are they confident about it? Most good creative teams are honest and will tell you when they're not sure. Which other routes did they explore? Why did they reject them?

When you find a strength in the work, you have a selling point which you can point out to the client. If you find a weakness in the work, tread carefully, it might call for attention. At all times, you should listen hard to the team's views. They've probably spent days working on it, and you probably haven't worked on the particular job since you put the brief in. They're employed for their creativity and judgement. Ignore this at your peril.

Occasionally, a weakness is just a misunderstanding. Even with clear briefing, it's still possible for creatives accidentally to get hold of the wrong end of the stick. Nobody minds making mistakes. In fact, if you get known as a good spotter of errors, especially on complex products, the creative team will regard you as an ally. (They don't want bad work appearing either.) Copywriters will show you pieces of copy before the creative director's seen them, asking you to check them for technical errors. You become a friend rather than a nit-picking enemy.

Most creative work has to run a long gauntlet before it can reach the customer. Your agency's creative director usually sits in judgement on all of his department's work, as do the account planner, the account director and other levels of account management, including yourself, as well as the client's organization. And sometimes the rough creative work is researched amongst groups of people selected from the target audience. This approval chain works well only if all concerned are either advertising experts who know what they are doing, or people who will allow themselves to be led into buying the creative solution. As long as you've got at least one good judge on any account, everyone else can happily be made to fall into line.

Finally, ask yourself whether the creative work meets the brief, and whether you can sell it to your client. (You might also consider the questions below.)

If you aren't convinced that the work should run, you should discuss your doubts with the creative team concerned: they might know something you've overlooked. And then maybe talk with a colleague. Incidentally, the best way to express *doubts* is often in the form of a question. For example, rather than committing yourself by saying 'I don't think this work is on strategy', ask others whether they think the work is on strategy. They'll probably ask you to remind them what the strategy is!

When you are convinced of the merits of the work, you should determine to sell it all the way through your agency and client organizations. Put a rocket behind it!

Advertising has to work hard to be successful. It must compete against editorial and other companies' advertising to get attention. It has to show the product's relevance and value, and usually either get remembered or lead to action. Safe advertising usually doesn't work particularly well.

When you look at a television idea you are usually looking at a storyboard: a series of pictures on a board, each of which represents a still frame of the intended commercial. Plus a written version of the soundtrack. Your storyboard must tell a story. The viewer must be able to make sense of your message through what he sees, as well as what he hears. Otherwise it's visual chaos. Television is drama. Viewers are most attentive at the beginning of each commercial and then their interest wanes. You must get them hooked at the outset.

Outstanding advertising provokes attention and is memorable. It's original enough to capture the attention of the audience. It will *interest* them. Each such advertisement normally contains an interesting idea, or a new twist to an old idea. All advertising contains a point of view on the product which, of course, it tries to show in a good light.

Keep a copy of the brief handy wherever you review creative work. And try asking these questions about each advertising idea presented to you.

1. Where's the proposition? (Is it up front or buried in the copy?)
2. Is the idea likely to get attention (from the agreed target audience)?
3. Does the idea provide a reason to read/watch?
4. Are the words in the customer's culture/language (or are there terms and expressions he's not already familiar with)?
5. Will the audience be able to relate to the visual style? (What will they make of it?)
6. *What* makes the idea different?
7. Will it be talked about? (By whom?)
8. What is exciting about the idea?
9. Will it be remembered? (What for?)
10. Can we prove our claims? (Are we making any?)
11. Will the idea make the customer do what we want him to do?
12. Has anything similar already been done? (Will our ad look the same?)

13. What will it look like in the media? Is it in the right size? (Does it need more space? Would it work as well in a smaller size?)

14. Does it help to develop the brand? (Or does it undermine its values?)

15. Can we afford to spend more time developing the idea?

You must also consider whether the idea is right for your particular client. Apart from the question of whether or not it *feels* right for your client, there is the issue of houserules or corporate identity guidelines. Most big companies and most mature advertisers have them. Just in case you're not familiar with them, here's an indication of the kind of thing covered in a 'Worldwide Identity Standards Manual', or rulebook, for short.

1. A definition of the kind of brand image that all of the company's advertising is designed to build, e.g. 'a caring company which always delivers quality'.

2. The relative weights of type, whether bold or not, and the amount of spacing between lines of text.

3. The size of the advertising, e.g. 'We always buy pages, nothing smaller. We want to look big'.

4. Whether photography or illustration is to be used, and if so which, so that all of one advertiser's advertisements might contain photographs while another uses illustrations.

5. The relative proportions of illustration and type and even the basic layout e.g. 'Photographs will appear at the top of each advertisement and the headline immediately underneath'.

6. Whether colour is to be used, and whether black and white is acceptable.

7. Whether the advertiser's name is to appear in the headline, and where his logo is to feature, if at all.

All of these rules are important because your client's advertising should be instantly recognizable as his – even when you take away the company name. If it looks like the competition, it may be helping the competition.

Rules help branding. True, in laying down branding rules you limit your creative options, and can make some otherwise sound ideas unworkable. But branding helps each advertisement reinforce all the others.

Does it look right?

The look of an advertisement can make or blight a strong creative idea. Good art direction is often critical, so you should always look for the best visual presentation of each creative idea. Indeed, an advertisement's looks imply a great deal about the advertiser. They can show class, friendliness, or sophistication – in fact, almost any quality at all. And you must consider what any particular treatment will do to your audience.

Visual styles have practical consequences. With a press advertisement, for example, ask yourself whether it leads you into the copy so that the sales pitch proper can start. You must always keep in mind how the finished version is likely to look.

Art directors vary in their visual literacy. Some are technically good but weak on ideas, and some are ideas men whose visual sense may be little above average. Some are over-fussy, and complicate the ideas they create. Other confuse advertising with art. (Advertising is about selling.) Of course, some are geniuses.

Every account handler should try to develop his visual senses. *Looking* at advertisements will help. So might visiting art galleries.

Handling check

1   Is the idea visually presented in a good way?
2   Is it right for the media environment you're planning?
3   Is it exciting enough to get attention?
4   Does it suggest the right things about the advertiser (e.g. class, speed of service or authority)?
5   Does it look contrived? (Is it over-fussy?)
6   Where will the reader's/viewer's eye start?
7   And where will he finish?
8   Does the layout take you into the copy? Will it work with the voice-over?
9   Does it obey all of the client's rules about his advertising's visual look?
10   How will the finished version be produced?
11   What will that look like?
12   How much will it cost to produce the advertisement in that way?
13   How long is it going to take to make?
14   Does the art director know who he wants to do the photography/direction and how they'll treat it? (Have you seen their work and is it consistent with your brand's values?)

How does your copy flow?

Good advertising copy *sells*. It's inviting, persuasive and easy to read. What makes a good piece of copy, and how can you judge whether it will work?

Copy should treat the reader or listener as an individual – an audience of one – and avoid talking as though it's addressing a crowd. It's written from the reader's (or viewer's) point of view, rather than the advertiser's. And it communicates the product's benefits.

What the customer needs to know may not tally with what the client wants to say. Too bad. The prospective customer (prospect, for short) is your important person. If the copy is filled with things your customer doesn't give a hoot about, he won't read your advertisement. Equally, if it omits things he does need to know, your advertisement is unlikely to work – frustrating the advertiser. If your writer can make the prospect see clearly in his mind exactly what the product is, what good it is to him, and what will happen if he buys it, he's written a good piece of copy.

Copy should start with something that's interesting to the prospect. It doesn't *have* to explain the advertisement's headline straightaway. And an interesting opening should be followed by more interesting remarks. Ideally, the prospect should now be thinking to himself 'This sounds good', and 'Gosh, I never knew that', and 'That's better than I thought'.

The rest of the copy should be as long as it needs to be and as short as possible.

Handling check

1 Is the copy clear? (If it isn't, there's no point in accepting it.)
2 Does it look interesting? (Will the potential reader be interested to read on?)
3 Is any part of it confusing or liable to leave viewers/readers with unanswered questions? (Will these questions encourage or put off the audience?)
4 Is it difficult to follow? (Does it use advertiser's jargon?)
5 Can any of it be cut? (Are there redundant phrases?)
6 Does the copy tell people what they are supposed to think about the product? (What does the tone of the copy imply about the advertiser? Is it pompous, patronizing or ponderous?)

7 Does it talk *to* you or *at* you? (Does it speak to you as an individual or as a public meeting?)
8 Does the copy keep your interest?
9 Does it cover all the points?
10 Is everything in the right order?
11 Does it *sell* the product? (Does it need to?)
12 Have you checked the obvious? (Address/name/phone number/telex/grammatical errors/spelling mistakes?)

Would some research help?

In the end, you have to rely on judgement as to what advertising should run. However, it's often worth trying to find out what effect any advertising might have by testing it amongst consumers.

The objective of such research could be to evaluate alternative advertising routes (in which case as little as one idea representing each route might be shown), or to establish the likely effects of one campaign or commercial. However, the big problem with such research is that most advertising is designed to work over time. A new strategy may well be designed to last for years. But in research, you can usually only measure a prospect's first reactions in one evening. Usually, the research can only tell you about people's *initial* reactions. You have to judge whether these reactions will last.

Normally, several group discussions with about half a dozen potential consumers would take place, each led by an agency planner or an outside researcher. Where necessary, for example in dealing with senior businesspeople, the interviews can be one-to-one and held at the interviewee's premises to save time.

The group leader will try to see what the advertising does to the group members, what it suggests to them about the product, and whether they find it credible. He'll also ascertain whether they like it and how their reactions compare with the advertising objective and the intended brand positioning. Whatever else a piece of research does, it will at least tell you whether your target market gets out of the work what you *think* you've put into it.

There are some drawbacks to research with small discussion groups. They can be dominated by one person (however hard the researcher tries to stop this) and not reflect the true views of the other people. They may be an odd group (it occasionally happens), and thus not reflect your target market accurately. You should use research as an aid to decisions, not as a crutch. It would be a pity if eight housewives in Neasden stopped a campaign to which the rest of Britain might respond.

Skipping on essential research can be costly. I once ran a press advertisement for a new client which was supposed to dominate its medium and bring a big response from retailers. It was one and a third pages big, and when it appeared in the trade newspaper it seemed to dominate the spread. When it generated just two responses, we felt we had to find out why. Five individual in-depth interviews with retailers were enough.

1. When we invited them to go through the issue of the paper in which the advertisement appeared, they were asked to comment on whatever caught their eye but not one of them stopped at or commented on our advertisement.

2. When we invited them to look at the advertisement, no interviewees noticed both sections of the advertisement. Nobody saw the extra third of the page.

3. None of them thought the advertisement was aimed at them, even though they all sold the product we were promoting. They thought we were addressing their customers, even though we were advertising in their trade paper.

4. None of them had heard of our client before, and they thought their customers would feel the same. They weren't about to start selling unknown brands, so they wouldn't have responded in any case.

5. None of them used coupons to respond for information although their newspaper was littered with them. They simply called up if they were interested.

Each of these problems – invisibility, incomprehensibility, irrelevance, total unfamiliarity and an inappropriate response mechanism – were sufficient to sink the campaign.

If we had proceeded without research, we might have changed the headline or the layout and tried again, wasting more money. Fortunately, advertising people learn quickly. With the benefit of research, we stopped advertising in that way. Research can save money and stop you producing bad advertising. Unfortunately, however, it's not sufficient to guarantee particularly good advertising.

And is it on strategy?

1   Is the work produced from the client's point of view or the customer's? (Who is it designed to impress, the client or the customer?)
2   Does it say what the advertiser wants to say or what the customer needs to know (before he'll do what we want)?
3   Are you taking into account what customers already know?
4   And what they don't know? (Are you using jargon? If so, why?)
5   Are you trying to say too many things in each advertisement? (Are you being single-minded about what you want to get across?)
6   Are you making claims for yourself without proving them?
7   Are you trying to spread the budget too thinly?
8   Should it be researched?

Chapter 10

Sell, sell, sell

Account handlers are salespeople. Your main job is to sell the agency's work. When you fail to make a sale, the creative or media work has to be done again, costing the agency time and therefore money. So good salesmanship is crucial to the agency's profits.

Few account handlers deliberately learn basic sales techniques. Any normal sales conversation can usefully include the following discrete stages:

1. Defining the client's needs.
2. Itemizing the benefits (of the agency's work for the advertiser).
3. Linking benefits with his needs.
4. Showing product fulfilment (how the idea works).
5. Handling objections.
6. Closing the sale.

Many account handlers believe they are natural salespeople. Some are.

How to sell good work

Like most salespeople, account handlers are often misunderstood. Selling is mostly about helping a potential buyer to identify his own needs and then showing him how you can help to fulfil them. It's also about handling his doubts regarding your product and closing the sale. Good selling makes buying easy.

Advertising really *isn't* about selling unwanted products at any cost. In fact, a first-rate advertising campaign can wreck a second-rate product. And if you force second-rate advertising upon your clients, you are likely to lose their business very quickly, while doing few favours to your agency along the way.

Your account handling faces its biggest test when you sell the agency's work. At this time, your ability to create the very best brief and motivate the creative team combine with the advertiser's trust and confidence in you. Will the combination work?

Presenting your advertising work should be a sales event in its own right. And you should show the work itself only when your client is warmed up and ready to buy it. Before doing so, you probably need to remind him of the advertising brief. And you'll need to explain why you've produced the work in the way that you have.

Going over the key points of the brief gets both your minds on what the work is supposed to achieve. Then you're in a good position to judge it. You should also mention any other relevant factors, from the levels of competitive activity to the choice of media. All this can be done briefly. By this point your client should be on the verge of buying the work, always providing that it meets the brief. The work itself simply proves the case you have made; it quietly completes the sale.

So once you've presented the work, and pointed to any interesting features, stop selling. Give your client some time to think. And buy.

Of course, selling isn't everything. I've heard it said that the secret of selling success comes in three parts. Find out what they want, find out how they want it, and then give it to them. However, if you apply this to your work as an account handler you'll probably end up with mediocre advertising and third-rate clients. The problem is that most advertisers want their agency's *judgement*. Indeed, that's usually why they hire an advertising agency. If your client already knows what he wants, the chances are that he can go up the road to a studio and get it produced, without all the hassle of using a full service agency.

Some of the most effective advertising took a great deal of selling. In some cases, it was turned down by the advertiser after the first meeting but resold at another. Good creative work can be difficult to appreciate. It usually isn't obvious that it's good on first sight. It can be difficult to sell.

A good account handler should not regard a thumbs-down from the client as necessarily being the end of the road for the work. It's an opportunity to pause and reflect, to reconsider the work's strengths and weaknesses, and to think through your client's concerns. If you still really believe in the work, your best route may be to go back to your client and explain to him why you are going to ask him (for a second time) to buy the work. This can be a heroic route, but it's often rewarding.

When work is turned down for a good reason, it's important that the client knows you understand and appreciate why, so that he feels you aren't going to make the same mistake again. Then, when you present fresh creative work, you should remind your client of the previous work, of why he turned it down, and explain that you've taken this into account in your new work.

Advertisers can find that turning down work becomes a habit. If you're not careful, your client will *expect* to find fault with your agency's work and substitute his judgement for yours. In the *long run* it's so much easier to apply your own judgement before your client sees it and bend every sinew to get the work you support approved by the client. Get it right and then get it sold. Regularly.

One of my all-time favourite advertising stories concerns selling, and may be found in full in *Madison Avenue, USA* by Martin Mayer. A new prospect asked Young and Rubicam what they would do if his company flatly rejected a proposed campaign. 'If you reject our best idea', the Y & R man said smoothly, 'we'll present our second-best idea.' The advertising manager was not satisfied, and asked what would happen if the company didn't like any of Y & R's ideas and insisted on having the campaign done its own way. 'Then we'll do it your way,' Y & R replied, 'because you might as well waste your money with us as with somebody else.'

Handling check

1 Before you ask a client to approve creative work do you remind him of the job the advertising has to do (the agreed objective)?
2 And what can be used to achieve it (the agreed strategy)?
3 Do you give the reasons why you've taken one creative route and, if relevant, why others won't work (creative decision-making)?

4   Do you reiterate any *relevant* agency prejudices to which the client isn't openly hostile (e.g. the need to dominate, be visible, single-minded)?

5   Have you made him feel excited about seeing the work?

6   Once you've shown it to him, do you take him through it and tell him why it works?

7   Are you prepared for his thoughts, ready to show you understand them, have taken them into account and perhaps even had the same thoughts yourself?

8   Can you successfully defend the work against most likely criticisms? (Try some out.)

So he didn't buy it

Good account handlers take responsibility for the success or failure of the agency's work, especially getting it sold to their clients.

Curiously, in some agencies the creative people have to present their own advertising work. Presumably the account handler just carries the bags. But let's assume it's normally up to the account handler to ensure the sale is closed, while the creative people get on and do more advertisements.

The account handler should know his client better than anyone else in the agency does. You are also at least partly responsible for the creative brief – you'll usually have signed it off – and for motivating the creative team to produce the work you present. So the buck stops with you. If your client won't buy your agency's work, consider the questions listed below.

Handling check

1   Is the work good enough? (If not you are at fault – you approved the work.)

2   Is the work off-brief? (You knew the brief and approved the creative work.)

3   Is the work right for the product, but done to the wrong brief? (You agreed the brief with the client.)

4   Is the client scared of buying the work? (He may need more persuasion, perhaps at another meeting.)

5   Are you selling the work hard enough? (Are you pointing to all its virtues?)

6   Are you selling it too hard? (Are you making unconvincing claims on its behalf?)

7   Does your client dislike the work? (If so, you may be at fault –
    you should find out what your clients like.)
8   Exactly why has the work been turned down?
9   What is the agency's point of view on what to do next?
10 How can this failure be prevented from happening again?
11 Do you blame the client when things go wrong? (Were you
    powerless?)
12 Do your colleagues think *you* are doing a good job?
13 Do *you* think you are doing a good job?

Are you selling bad advertising?

Some advertising is just plain bad: it doesn't work to achieve the
advertiser's objective. But why would an account handler allow or
even encourage bad work to be produced? It could be said that it's
because of the client.

It may happen something like this. Initially some good work is
turned down by the client, and then bad work is produced and
approved. After some experience of this, the agency decides to
present bad work to the client, to save time and effort. Both client
and agency are responsible for the work. So thereafter both client
and agency have to agree that the bad work was really quite good.
What else can they do?

Or could it be that everyone is doing one another's work. Lacking
a good brief, your creatives might spend such time as is available
working one out. And lacking well considered creative work, your
client might get personally involved in writing the copy. He might
enjoy it, but the formula is very unlikely to work.

Handling check

1   Is the advertising produced by the right people doing the wrong
    things?
2   Do you compliment the client's thinking instead of questioning
    it?
3   Do the creative team spend time trying to work out a brief for
    their creative work?
4   Does the client think he can (help) write the advertisement?
5   Should *you* really be working at this particular agency?

Chapter 11

Buy, buy, buy

Agencies buy audiences. Media are simply a way of getting to the target audience that the advertising is supposed to reach. And media buying can be a mean business. It's about delivering the target audience as cost-effectively as possible, and can involve aggressive negotiation to get the lowest possible rates or a more friendly, softly-softly approach. Good media buyers are usually *respected* by the media salespeople. But they're often not *liked* as much as the sloppy media buyers who buy spaces at the rates on each medium's published 'rate card'. Insist on the best deal.

As an account handler, you should aim to give your media buyer as much freedom to negotiate as possible. Then he can alternately tempt media with business and threaten them with no business if the rate doesn't drop low enough. And your buyer needs freedom to implement his threat from time to time. This increases his power to deliver the audience cheaply.

Buyers weave yarns. They tell the media salespeople that their client just might be interested, at the right price. Even when a publication is already on the intended schedule, they'll explain that the client's budget won't allow them to buy unless the medium reduces its prices, when, in fact, it's up to the buyers. And they'll argue that future media use may depend upon what is used this time around, so the price had better be right.

The best buyers are also careful about when they buy. They'll go hunting in the spaces other media buyers have overlooked, and they'll buy at the last minute. And if one medium fills up before they finally pounce, they will go elsewhere, or try another day.

More media planning

Planning is important too, even after the big decision has been taken on which kind of media your client should use. Once that main decision is made, your media planner must decide how to split the available budget between the different media.

He will consider coverage of the target audience and the frequency with which they'll be reached, as well as the cost per thousand people reached of doing so. Some agencies tend to go for as high a proportion of the target audience as possible. Others may customarily aim to concentrate their coverage sufficiently to ensure that they outspend the competition in those particular places, even at the expense of not reaching some people at all.

Which approach is more likely to work for you depends on the creative work. When is it likely to be at its best? After one, two or more outings? What is its optimum level of frequency of appearance? Additionally, it could be that a particular medium reaches a high proportion of your product's heavy users, supporting the focused strategy. All of these factors should be taken into account in the media plan.

How to review a media schedule

You should review the media plan and make sure you understand its logic before taking a view on it and presenting it to your client. Again, the crucial question is whether it answers the brief. Is it on strategy? And will it allow you to achieve the campaign's objectives?

You will need to talk it through with the media planner or buyer, check the assumptions he has made, and ascertain why one media solution has been preferred to another. He will attempt to:

Minimize the cost of reaching any given number of your audience. This measure is called 'cost per thousand'. Put around the other way, it also means maximizing the numbers (of thousands) of your audience for any given budget.

Maximize the coverage of your audience within the budget. This is expressed in percentage terms; a 60 per cent coverage means your plan reaches six out of ten members of your audience.

And maximize the number of times your audience is exposed to the advertising. This is called 'opportunities to see', or OTS for short. As a team, you'll take a view on how often a commercial or print advertisement needs to be seen in order for the campaign to work. And on the more sophisticated plans you might expect to see an indication of how the average OTS varies amongst your audience, i.e. how many would be exposed to it once, how many twice and so on.

Don't start off your review of the media schedule by discussing the individual recommended media. Instead, start off by discussing how the plan works in terms of the variables just mentioned. Look at the coverage achieved. Think about how the consumer is going to feel after he's been exposed to the creative work three times, if that's the average frequency. Consider whether he would be motivated enough to make a purchase.

Also think about what happens to the media mix if you change your brief at the margin. Is the schedule flexible enough to cope with a slightly different media brief? (Media briefs have a habit of changing as new customer information becomes available.) And what are the schedule's implications for production costs? Does it increase them over your previous estimates?

Do you know what happens at the end of the timeplan covered by the media schedule? Does this schedule anticipate a continuing presence or will it work as a stand-alone?

Handling check

1 What are the good features of the media plan?
2 Why is it ingenious?
3 Where are you outspending the competition, even on this budget? In the timing, e.g. day of the week? In a particular medium or position, e.g. dominance of outside back cover positions? Or a part of the country?
4 How can you dominate the target audience's mind? (By dominating the media – taking the biggest or best positions – and being noticed and remembered by the target audience?)
5 Or is the advertising idea so strong (or the objective so modest) that you don't need to dominate in any of these ways?

6 And how many exposures are needed?
7 What will be on the viewer's/reader's mind when he sees the advertisement (by virtue of the editorial, the time of day, what happened last week – e.g. the Budget, Christmas etc.)?
8 How does the media plan help the creative idea to work (e.g. by giving it dominance)?
9 What are the coverage and frequency figures?
10 Does it work as a stand-alone schedule?

Burst, pulse or flight?

It's only after your team have made the big media decision as to which kinds of media your campaign should run in, that you can brief your creative work (your creative people need to know whether they are working on a press campaign, for example). Then you can get on with the detailed work of media planning.

Timing issues need to be tackled. Some fundamental media principles have already been discussed and a few characteristics of different kinds of media.

Although account handlers should be able to rely on their media planners to provide a great deal of expertise, they should have a grasp of the issues that emerge at this point. One of the most important is the shape of the schedule over time. As there's no right answer which extends across all situations, several possibilities will be considered.

One option is to be an ever-present advertiser. But continuous advertising runs the risk of becoming invisible as people grow accustomed to it. It's also a very expensive way to advertise. It can be difficult to evaluate its effectiveness. And you don't get a chance to see what happens to sales when you stop advertising.

Another option is to run your advertising in one big burst or in a series of bursts. One big burst may give you the chance to outspend the competition for a short period of time, and even to dominate the medium in which your advertising appears. It also gives you a good chance to see what effect the advertising has upon sales (or whatever else you are trying to affect). But it can leave your client's campaign looking like a flash in the pan, here today and gone tomorrow.

The fact is, people forget most of what they learn within a day. But most of what they remember for a week or so is likely to stay with them for a long time. If pressed, they can recall it.

Running a series of bursts is sometimes called 'flighting'. Sometimes you're there and sometimes you're not. And then you come back again. It's a strategy used by some politicians, including the current Prime Minister, Mrs Thatcher. She'll aim to have a high presence in the media, as far as possible on her own terms, for 2–3 weeks and then aim for a low profile for a similar time period. This can maximize impact, and minimizes boredom.

You might feel, however, that you can't entirely disappear from the market. Then, 'pulsing' is a subtler strategy. In pulsing you alternate high levels of expenditure with relatively low levels, but you never disappear altogether.

Of course, it could be that you need to start your campaign with a big burst and then switch to some pulsing, after which you do some flighting and then stop. Anything's possible. And there are no set rules.

How to buy people cheaply

Most advertising media have a salesforce who have their own sales targets to reach. And they are usually remunerated through a mixture of salary and commission on sales.

The smallest or most specialist media share salesforces with one another, or use independent salespeople who may represent a string of publications. The big media allow their salesforce to specialize. Each salesperson may deal with a particular kind of advertiser or product, or with a shortlist of advertising agencies. He tries to get to know them well.

Luckily you don't have to get involved in media buying too often. You should aim to give your media buyers as much freedom as possible. Then they can negotiate without having their hands tied behind their backs. This can be difficult if they're not on the spot.

Recently a client of mine wanted to appear in the following weekend's press. With three days to go we had no spaces. Some of the papers were full and others wouldn't reduce their rate to a price that the buyer felt happy about. On Thursday, with two days to go, the media buyer was away at a new business pitch and his assistant, who was going to buy the press, was ill. So I instructed another media buyer to get some spaces in the positions we wanted at the best available price. By Friday morning, we had got some spaces.

The client was still upset that we didn't get into all the newspapers he wanted. (He really didn't care about the price; we did.) But he was not nearly as upset as he would have been if he had no media reserved at all.

The account's media buyer, back from the pitch, was *really* upset. I had ruined his buying record by allowing the agency to buy spaces at higher rates than he would have accepted, thus setting a precedent for his future purchases. He felt I should have held out until Friday morning before buying, to see what was available in the market.

Sometimes your media buyer doesn't want to hear about your client's perspective and sometimes your client doesn't want to hear about your media department's view. You've got to reconcile the two.

Handling check

1   Do your media buyers know exactly what you want and when?
2   And what can change (and by how much) and what can't (e.g. day of the week, size/length, age profile)?
3   And how much latitude they can have (e.g. on the sizes they can buy)?
4   Are your media being bought at the cheapest possible price, i.e. with the largest discount against the medium's rate card?
5   Are you allowing your buyers enough flexibility on day, week, positions and choice of media?
6   And are they able to respond quickly to short-term media offers, whether or not the client is around at the time?
7   Have you got the client used either to taking decisions quickly or leaving these decisions to the agency?
8   Do your buyers have the freedom to say no to particular offers and take a chance on whether a better price will be offered?
9   Or do you expect them to feign lack of interest in a particular media proposition but subsequently have to give in?
10 Is your agency's production department being kept informed of all bookings?

Chapter 12

Into production

Fortunately, the account handler doesn't have to produce finished advertising. There's someone to help you at every stage, even though you remain responsible for the work. And production's where things can go seriously wrong, and in a costly way.

At least three problem areas can emerge after the concepts, storyboards and/or copy are agreed by the agency and the client: these concern timing, costs, and quality of work. And they apply to television commercials as well as print advertising, outdoor posters and radio.

The agency business usually works *to* deadlines, not *within* them. This makes any production process difficult: lose time at any of the stages of production and you may not be able to make it up if your timing is tight. In theory, the answer is simple: build spare time into the process at the end of your schedule, and strongly resist all demands to fritter away that margin of error. Just like a good driver who'll keep his distance from the car in front of him, a good account handler will always keep some time up his sleeve. It gives him room for manoeuvre.

Costs will concern most of your clients. Advertisers want to know that their money isn't being wasted, or simply disappearing within the agency or its suppliers. Their concern can sometimes be well-founded, so the client's account handler should be concerned first.

You should satisfy yourself that production costs are as low as they ought to be, and you should ask all the questions you feel are necessary. Only this way can you earn the advertiser's trust.

Production costs can seem very high, especially for making television commercials. But it's often a mistake to try to force costs down and it's always a mistake to pretend that they're going to turn out lower than they will, as the following cautionary tale shows.

An agency once pitched for an account. The creative work centred round a very strong TV commercial set in evocative outdoor surroundings. The agency loved the commercial. The client also fell in love with it and awarded the agency the business.

A conversation follows in the agency, when the delighted creative people hear that their potentially prize-winning commercial is going to be made:

Creative:	Great! When's it wanted?
Handler:	Well, it won't be running till December, but we want it months earlier for their sales conference.
Creative:	Never mind, summer's running out, we need daylight anyway.
Handler:	The budget's not very big.
Creative:	We'll manage somehow. What's 'not very big'?
Handler:	It's not a big media spend.
Creative:	What's the production budget?
Handler:	I have a figure of £20,000.
Creative:	What? What production company quoted you that?
Handler:	£20,000 is all the client can afford.
Creative:	You can't even shoot a still table-top for £20,000, let alone have actors. And sound. And location. What deal have you done with someone?
Handler:	Well, I haven't actually spoken to a production company.
Creative:	But you had the script a fortnight before the pitch. You must have got that figure from somewhere.
Handler:	The client was very happy with the figure.
Creative:	So I should think! £60,000 would be cheap. Where did you get that figure from? LONG SILENCE
Handler:	I made it up. I didn't want us to seem expensive . . .

Budgets are serious business. Being honest about budgets means facing up to problems before they get out of hand.

Good creative work can be compromised by poor finishing. Concern about costs can get out of proportion, unnecessarily weakening the advertising, and getting in the way of your colleagues' efforts. Quality account handlers sell quality budgets.

How to produce print advertisements

Print advertisements are almost the simplest form of advertising. They're also amongst the most difficult to do well. They can vary from black and white copy-only press advertisements to full-colour photographic spreads. You may not have been lucky enough to start with the simplest kind of production jobs. I did, but it didn't help much.

One of the first advertisements I ever handled was a 'bearer notice' to stockholders of a mining company. It was going to appear in both the *Financial Times* Company Notices column and the *Daily Telegraph* in a space about 10 centimetres deep and just one column wide. But I still managed to get it wrong.

All I had to do was get the wording from the client and send copies to those two newspapers marked 'set in 6 point across one column to depth' and attach the company logo and a copy of the last 'bearer notice' as a guide for style to show the printers at the newspapers which lines would be set in capitals, where the address lines should go, and so on. They would type out my words to form metal characters for reproduction. Anyway, somehow or other, one of the newspapers carried the advertisement without the mining company's logo. It seemed that I hadn't instructed them to put the logo in.

It was my first week at the agency. The client was upset and demanded a free repeat appearance. And I was worried. The agency's media director came in to reassure me. I must have looked awful. He said, 'Look, what's the worst thing that could happen to you now?' I couldn't answer. 'All they could do is fire you.' And he was trying to reassure me! Three years later, *he* was fired. Which might go to show that if you are a media director, you shouldn't talk about your agency as 'they'.

Today, you'd be hard pressed to find yourself in an agency producing advertisements which are sent to the newspapers for setting. Higher standards and professional typesetting have meant that the habit has almost died out.

So how do you handle the production of a press advertisement today? Let's start with the simplest case. Suppose your client has just cleared an all-type advertisement. The layout and copy are approved and so is your production estimate for making the advertisement. What happens next?

You need an approved media schedule. And unless your production department knows where the advertisements are going to appear, they can't make the necessary material. Each medium has its own requirements. They need their own kind of material. For example, even national daily newspapers have slightly different column widths. A page in the *Daily Mail* isn't the same size as a page in the *Daily Express*.

You'll also need to tell your production department where within the paper the advertisement is scheduled to appear, as, for example, the thickness of paper can vary within one printed medium and this affects how you produce material. Some pages reproduce colour well and some don't, and so on. And you should tell production where on the page the advertisement is going to appear (if the advertisement is smaller than a page). A left-hand edge booking for a couponed advertisement means that the coupon should appear in the bottom left-hand corner.

Your art director will have done a rough of the advertisement, showing approximately where the headline goes and where the body copy goes, and so on. Before setting the advertisement, you probably need to instruct the production house on *exactly* where the copy should run and in what size, and so on. Unless you want to leave it to them.

This instruction is done visually. It's called a type mark-up, or 'TMU', for short. In large advertising agencies, this job is usually done by people who specialize in type and design. For understandable reasons they're called typographers. Smaller agencies usually don't have typographers in-house, in which case your art director will probably instruct the setting house himself.

A good typographer can make an average advertising idea look super. Even in a simple case, the typographer's job includes working out exactly where the type will go. Printed type comes in specified sizes which are called point sizes. The typographer can vary the amounts of spacing or 'leading' (pronounced ledding) between lines. Typographers have to count the letters, each of which is called a character, and partially trace over, to see exactly where the copy will fall. Then, when the setting comes back from the setting house (usually the following morning), it should look good because the right instructions will have been given.

What comes in from the supplier in the morning is known as an 'artwork' if it's an original, or even a 'mechanical artwork' or 'mech' for short, if it's on a board with a flip card cover to protect it. Often you just see a copy of this, and 'imitation artwork' (abbreviated to 'IA'), or, more simply, just a proof. In some agencies you'll only get a photocopy of the artwork. It's cheap, and it'll do for copy checking purposes.

Anyway, you check your proof against the original copy that the client approved. The best system is that one person reads out from the approved copy, while another follows on the proof, marking any errors. The person calling out needs to say, 'Cap T The person . . .' verbally describing when capitals should be used.

Your art director should check one of these proofs from a visual point of view: has it come out the way he wanted it to? And your writer should double-check the copy. Often the copy needs to be adjusted at this stage. For instance, to allow the words to work their way evenly around a photograph, or to avoid having the last word of a paragraph sitting uncomfortably on its own.

If your colleagues are happy with it, they approve the setting by signing off on the artwork or a proof, depending on the agency's system. (Some agencies don't have a signing-off system, and some people don't like the responsibility of signing off, but it makes mistakes less likely.)

If your colleagues have signed off, you probably want to get a proof to the client. Actually, you probably wanted to get it to your client hours before your colleagues signed it off! If the setting needs revision (and it normally does), you might hold off sending it to the client, or you might send him a copy with the changes you plan to make marked upon it. Then you'll incorporate the agency's changes and any others you agree into the second proof.

Whether or not you send an uncorrected first proof off to your client depends on how much time you have, on whether the first proof reflects badly on the agency in any way – could the agency have done a better TMU? – and on what your client is like. Some don't want to see any proofs, except the one that the agency has approved and is happy to run, others like to get closely involved in every aspect of the job.

This process of proofing and re-proofing can go on for a surprising length of time. Suppose that on the first day a copy error is spotted. You revise the setting. On the second day, your art director wants to change something. You revise the setting again. But it still isn't right. Revise the setting once more. Then the client wants to change a couple of things. Revise the setting a fourth time. Then his boss does. Revise the setting a fifth time. Then his lawyers do. Revise the setting again. Then your art director has another thought. Revise the setting a seventh time. And so it goes on, running up a big production bill, unless you work hard to avoid it. Half a dozen proofings are not uncommon.

Whether your client's verbal approval will do before you sign off an advertisement and release it to the media or whether you need his signature, is a matter of judgement. It depends on the client.

The addition of illustrations or of photography, and even colour, doesn't affect the account handler's life as much as you might think. But they are more fun for your art director. The principles remain the same, although you'll have to check colour proofs from each publication.

Your art director gets to hire an illustrator or photographer and he spends time going through their portfolios. You might want to be involved in this selection process, but you probably don't have the time. And anyway, it's up to him. If there's photography, your art director will probably go to the photographic shoot to ensure that he gets the picture he wants.

Before he briefs this task out, he'll do a rough of the visual showing what he wants and where, and he'll also have a visual reference showing the style of visual he's looking for. It may be a good idea to see these before the work itself is done, just to check that you won't be unpleasantly surprised later, and to talk it over with the art director. Is the client going to buy this? Should you tell him exactly what you're up to or surprise him with the completed work? Surprises are risky. Some clients like to go to photographic shoots. That's risky too. But if they go, you've got to be there.

You'll see the photographic prints a day or two after the shoot and your art director may choose one to progress for use. Even his chosen shot may need work done to it, lightening, darkening or just plain altering, usually called retouching; or he may want to take a bit of one photograph and a section of another and do a 'photo-comp', which as far as you're concerned means they get stuck together to look like one photograph. But it may bust your production budget, so be careful.

When work on the visual draws to a conclusion you'll probably want to get your words set in the usual way. Once they're right, a complete advertisement can be created for signing off.

Although posters are quite different from newspapers and magazines from a creative point of view – you've got about a second to get your message over – in production terms they're quite similar. You normally have to go to a particular poster site in order to see the finished thing. Some agencies have such sites on top of their buildings, others have them in their car parks. Others don't have them in-house.

Things can go wrong with poster production too. One client was going outdoors on one special poster site only. And it was going to be one big illustration. The cheapest way to do one poster was to have it painted rather than printed. So we did. But that month it rained and rained. And even our 'waterproof' paint began to run.

Broadcasting the work

Radio is pretty simple for account handlers. You are only dealing in sound. Your creative team can have recordings done, listen as they're happening, hear them straight afterwards again and again, and edit away to their heart's content for quite small sums of money.

One problem with radio is time. If you are buying 30-second slots, your commercial must run for just under 30 seconds. Your script must therefore be written to length, including time for any sound effects. Having just one or two words too many can force your 'voice' to speak too quickly. You can't run over time. One way to get round this problem of running over is to play the tape back slightly faster to get within the time. The sound gets slightly higher, but it needn't be noticeable.

Television is more complex. It's easy to let the costs get out of control, and the timing. You've got pictures and movement and sound, usually including words, all of which have to be approved by the ITV Association (formerly known as the ITCA). The script needs to be cleared before you start shooting.

TV generates more, and bigger, meetings (costs are high, media expenditure will be high, so it's more important to everybody). Pre-shoot meetings take a lot of time and a lot of co-ordination. Fortunately, account handlers don't have to know how to make television commercials. But there are your copywriter and art director, there's the chosen director who is in charge when the cameras are rolling, just like in the movies (he probably works in feature films too), there are his cameramen whom he works with, discussing angles and so on, there's at least one sound man, sitting there with headphones on, there's a lighting man or two, a few actors and the occasional agent. In addition, there's someone for make-up, someone for props, someone to move them around, the producer, someone from the agency's TV and production departments, someone who's learning the ropes, someone to make tea, the odd secretary, the client and you, and all those people who want to see how a commercial is made. And you're all keeping very, very quiet. That's just for a very simple, short commercial, and I've probably left some people out.

Anyway, the director probably won't listen to anyone except, occasionally, the agency's TV producer, art director and copywriter. So if you or the client have got anything to say, you've got to have a quiet word with these people. They'll probably do take after take until it's the best they think it can be. As a rule, they'll use the time available to them to make it the best possible advertisement.

Outdoor shoots usually call for weather insurance. Rain could cost you a fortune with all those people sitting around, but the weather insurance premium may cost half a fortune. If you're using well-known actors you've got to consider cover against their dying before the commercial finishes running, or falling into disrepute in a way that makes them unsuitable to promote your client's product. Insurance is safe. Either way you should get the client's agreement.

After the shoot, the first thing your creatives see is the 'rushes', the uncut bits of film from the shoot including the best takes of each cinema shot. A production company will work with your art director and copywriter to piece your commercial together in the best way. Editing time costs money too, so keep watching the budget. And captions get stuck on last.

It's up to you whether the client sees the rough cut which consists of the best of all the takes stuck together. If your client isn't happy with the resulting work to the extent that you need a reshoot, you've both got a very big problem.

Handling check

1 Does *everyone* concerned know how much time is available to finish the work? (Have you built in a margin for stoppage/doing work again?)
2 Is there an agreed timetable?

3 Is the budget known?
4 Have you taken competitive quotes at each stage?
5 And chosen the best *value* one (not necessarily the lowest prices)?
6 Has your client approved the quotes and the timing?
7 Has he agreed to pay weather insurance or simply pray?

Chapter 13

Will it do the job?

What makes a success

Advertising should work. It should achieve the objectives that are set for it. The only valid way to test advertising is against the objectives set. To measure its success against anything else is to 'move the goalposts' during the process, making it difficult for the agency to score!

However, it can be difficult to isolate the effects of advertising from other factors, like the quality of the product, distribution, promotions and competitive activity. And even when it can be done, what worked last time may not work next time. And what *failed* last time might, in different circumstances, work next time.

Nevertheless, the advertiser and agency can extend the life of a campaign that works, and make an initial success into a bigger one. Finding out what works also helps improve everybody's judgement. One of the best ways for an account handler to develop his judgement is to watch his campaign working, or failing to work.

Before you run the campaign itself, you should have a clear idea of what constitutes success. For that to be meaningful, you must also know how you are going to measure it. And you should agree goals with your client. Otherwise, there's every possibility that you could subsequently be congratulating yourself and your colleagues on the successes of the campaign while your client is upset by its apparent failure.

The simplest measurement is often sales. It's also the least contentious. If you can divide your audience into two identical groups, one of which is exposed to the advertising and one of which is not, and then measure their purchases before and after the advertising runs, you'll be able to establish the net effect of the advertising by looking at how the exposed group have changed their buying habits, in comparison with the unexposed.

This can be revealing. There's a famous story about one major advertiser who split-ran their advertisements in *Reader's Digest* so that half the readers were regularly exposed to their campaign over one year, and one group not at all. At the end of the year, the group who had *not* been exposed to their advertising proved to be more likely to buy their merchandise. Their advertising had actually had a negative effect!

In any event, it's critical to measure sales before and after advertising, in a meaningful way. If you can't run an advertising split-sales test, you'll have to resort to trying to isolate the effects of distribution, seasonal factors, in-store and competitive activity, which is very difficult and often impossible.

Apart from testing creative work, you might well want to test the relative effectiveness of different media strategies. Bursts, pulses and flights are all discussed in Chapter 11 on media buying. Their relative effectiveness can be tested. If you run the same creative work in, say, each region but vary the media strategy, you can run with the more effective media strategy in the second phase of the campaign, thus saving your client's money.

The best basis on which to judge whether or not a campaign will work is to use your own judgement. If you aren't sure about the value of a campaign, you can use research.

Print advertisements and commercials can be pre-tested without incurring large production costs. For example, you can make slides or a rough drawn version of your proposed commercial, called an animatic and test this rough version in front of an audience. This will help establish whether the commercial gets across what you are trying to communicate. It's a forced viewing test and it won't tell you whether anyone will notice the commercial at all. But it will tell you what they take from it if they do notice it.

In order to test whether anyone notices it you've really got to run the commercial for real, against other television material, including competitive commercials. This is often done through what is called an on-air recall test. You put the commercial on air in one region and then, 24 hours later, telephone viewers to see which commercials they recall and what they took from your own. In this case you incur the cost of making a commercial and some media costs, together with research costs too. But you do very quickly gain an idea of how the commercial is being received (if not how people will act on it) which will help you with the rest of the campaign.

Handling check

1 Will you measure pre and post-campaign sales?
2 Will you measure sales in both advertised and non-advertised regions?
3 And awareness and loyalty? Are the advertisements going to be direct-response?
4 Are you split-running the press advertisements (different advertisements in alternate copies of a paper)?
5 Can you take account of distribution, seasonal factors, in-store and competitive activity when you try to isolate the effects of the advertising?
6 Will you learn whether a heavyweight media burst works better than a lighter but longer drip plan? (Did you already know?)
7 Will you be able to see whether advertising expenditure and sales move together over time?

Why review the campaign?

Advertisers get exposed to their own advertising again and again. Consumers see it more rarely. In fact, clients often see the advertising idea long before it starts running, and can grow tired of it even before it sees the light of day! It's old hat to the advertiser.

Although advertising usually produces some quick results, it can also cause longer-term effects, especially if it gets remembered. It can promote the product or brand's personality. And as the advertising builds personality, so the brand can become its customers' friend. A new campaign can destroy that relationship.

Advertising campaigns get changed pretty quickly, typically in one to two years. But some campaigns go on working for decades. Not surprising, then, that they're amongst the most famous. Very often, you've got to resist the urge to kill the goose that lays the golden egg. Let's consider some of the possible *reasons* for killing a campaign.

Suppose your client's sales are dropping. Is the advertising at fault? Possibly. But it may be that the quality of your client's product has fallen behind the competition, or that there's a distributional problem, or that too little is being spent on advertising.

When could it be the case that a campaign which used to work needs to be changed? It could be that it's culturally out of date. If it was devised in the 1960s, it could well be too dated for the 1980s. But good advertising ideas can usually be brought up to date without being chopped altogether. Update the campaign if possible, don't drop it.

Or it could be that the product has evolved to such an extent that the campaign's central promise is no longer appropriate. Or that the product's audience, which likes the campaign, are numerically too small and you now need to strike out and reach new groups. Maybe you need a new campaign to reach *them*. But a major change may decrease the loyalty of your product's existing audience.

Or perhaps the competition have come up with a better advertising campaign which is taking your client's business away. Maybe they have a better product. Maybe their idea can only work in the short run. Maybe your own campaign wasn't so good after all. Even then, it might be better to stick with it than to change again.

Dropping an advertising campaign is not therefore a decision to be taken lightly. Anyway, it's much better to get it right first time round.

Handling check

1   Is the campaign being reviewed because the client has grown tired of it?
2   Or because a new brand manager wants to make a brand new start?
3   Or because the agency wants to prove that it can come up with new ideas?
4   Has the customer grown tired of the campaign?
5   Or is someone trying to justify himself?

Part III
The rest

Chapter 14

How to support the campaign

Advertising agencies are in business to produce advertising. In doing so, you could see other ways to help your client. Your advertising idea might work well in a leaflet. You might think it worthwhile to mail some customers. The advertising campaign might be worth telling journalists about. A sponsorship opportunity might help the creative work to go further.

You could provide this kind of help simply in order to build goodwill. Or you might charge for it, depending on how much the client's business is worth to the agency. Either way, these possibilities can often be worth some serious thought.

The line

An advertising agency's raison d'être is to produce effective advertising. This doesn't mean that the solutions to the problems you encounter are confined to the traditional advertising media we've already discussed. The solutions can extend into related fields. You can get involved in these areas too.

'Above-the-line' work ——	Advertising media e.g. TV, radio, press, magazines, posters.
'Below-the-line' work ——	Print, videos, design work, direct mail, public relations, sponsorship, new product development.

Work on which agencies traditionally take a commission is above-the-line. The rest is below-the-line work.

There can be a logic to advertising agencies getting involved in these different areas. Some clients like to buy a number of services through one agency rather than several. They may reduce their agency liaison time, and by pooling their promotional wants in one agency, they can become a more important client to the agency. Agencies, for their part, can grow more quickly by cross-selling additional non-advertising services to existing clients and by helping the client to ensure that all the different communications techniques work together. Some are tempted.

However, advertising is a specialist business, and most mature clients are able to provide their own integration. These clients aim to buy the best advertising from the best advertising agencies, while buying below-the-line services from other specialists. So far, specialists have tended to excel. What follows are simply some notes about below-the-line work which might come in handy. They fall far short of enabling you to do-it-yourself.

Advertising by mail

Direct mail is arguably more like mainstream advertising than other below-the-line areas. It's simply advertising by post or hand delivery. Indeed, it is sometimes called 'direct mail advertising'.

Sometimes advertising problems can be solved by direct mail

more cost-effectively than through other advertising media. Its main advantage is that it can be far more selective than other media. You can write to dentists in Halifax, for example, and your message can be specifically tailored to them. The direct mail industry has its own guidelines for producing effective mailings, each of which tends to include the following four basic items:

1. a letter, which may well be personalized, i.e. the intended recipient is addressed by name, and the letter is usually signed off in blue ink;

2. a brochure which goes into more detail about the product or service being offered;

3. a response device, like a pre-paid response card bearing the return address;

4. the envelope, which creates the first impression with the receiver and can be personalized.

One set of guidelines is summed up by the acronym SNOUCE which argues that successful mailings are:

●*specific* in the offer they make to customers
●*newsworthy*
●make a good *offer*
●for a *unique* product or service
●are *creatively* produced
●and make it *easy* for people to respond.

All these features help make a success.

On the whole, direct mailers are trying to generate an immediate response and close a sale, rather than build a brand. The objective of the mailing could be to maximize orders for a demonstration or to sell the service immediately. In either case the customer has to be almost completely sold on the product before he will react.

Another acronym has been invented to describe the *stages* in this selling process. AIDA stands for the following:

1. first, you must get the reader's *attention*;

2. then, you start to *interest* him in the product;

3. next, through showing its benefits you build his *desire* to own the product;

4. until it has grown sufficiently for him to want to take *action*.

In fact, there's far too much jargon in direct mail!

Your success in direct mail depends critically upon your mailing list. Specialist list-building organizations exist which will rent or sell you one of their lists. Most of them cost £25–£100 per thousand names and addresses, to rent. Usually you can have the list in the form of sticky labels for application to envelopes which might be convenient if you are not planning to personalize the material which goes inside, or on computer tape. The list companies usually insert a number of their own house names onto each list you rent, so that they can find out if you cheat and continue to use their list when you hired it only for a particular use in the first place. Other organizations will gladly handle the compilation of material, envelope stuffing, address writing and dispatch.

Incidentally, you can negotiate cheap postal rates with the Post Office on large mailings. They are keen to attract the business and have set up an organization called the Direct Mail Sales Bureau to help advertisers and agencies.

However, the trouble with lists is that they vary in quality, and the best ones have usually been extensively used by the competition. And they decay quickly as people move. Even so, most direct mail is not thrown away. At least, not immediately. A private, purpose-built mailing list can be worth its weight in gold.

Handling check

1   Have you considered the merits of direct mail as an alternative medium?
2   Have you thought through how direct mail can contribute to the campaign?

Sponsoring Events

Your client might want to get famous fast, or to be seen as a lively, young or sporting company, or as an artistic company or one that's socially concerned. Sponsorship or charitable donations could help achieve some of these goals.

For a sum of money to be agreed, it is now possible to associate companies or boards with most sporting and cultural events. Your client can get his company or brand name across in a big way. If the event embodies the values with which your client wants to be associated, the case for sponsorship is stronger; otherwise its main value is to increase name awareness.

This can cause problems. On occasion companies have become known mainly for their sporting connections, while their product remained largely unknown. Usually, awareness increases fast in the first year or two of association, but then plateaus quite quickly. Some clients find that sponsorship brings a big increase in awareness but they have not worked out how to translate that into extra sales.

Relating to the public

Advertising is usually concerned with sales. Public relations is concerned with building bridges between a company and its various target audiences – what the PR people like to call their 'publics'.

Advertising is, of course, the most visible part of many companies' public relations processes. Certainly, the advertising industry is much bigger than the whole of the public relations industry. And advertising agencies tend to own public relations agencies, rather than the other way round.

Of course, a company's advertising does not take place in a vacuum. It is usually devoted to persuading an audience of the merit of something. Whether or not persuasion takes place and is lasting depends on many other factors. Through public relations, companies attempt to influence some of them.

Good public relations can help an advertising campaign to succeed. Bad public relations can certainly get in the way of its success. Yet from an account handling point of view, the two crafts – advertising and public relations – are quite different. In fact, PR agencies are likely to get involved in a miscellany of related fields. From developing relations with journalists in television, the national and international press, radio and the specialist trade press, to answering customers' complaints, and from conferences to sponsorship – anything that might help a company's relations with the public.

Your advertising can help to generate editorial coverage. Advertising campaigns are usually news events in their own right, at least for the retail trade. Their launch can act as a peg for journalists to hang stories on, or cause them to consider writing about the company. Thus, advertising campaigns can help create good public relations. Advertising is a high-profile activity. The relevant journalists may need to be serviced with the appropriate background material so that their articles are supportive of the advertiser, rather than critical. Advertising account handlers should ensure that their clients have covered the PR angle. The agency will also need to agree with the client when the relevant trade press should be informed of advertising activity, and what should be said about it.

If a particular advertiser's objective really can be achieved by clearly and regularly communicating with a few dozen journalists, he needn't advertise at all. By comparison, advertising will probably be more expensive.

Handling check

1   How can the campaign be used to help the advertiser's editorial coverage?
2   What sort of write-up does the advertising campaign need, and from whom?

Hitting them where they buy

Apart from the product packaging itself, your client probably promotes his goods at the places where they are sold. This is called point-of-sale material. It includes shelf strips, posters, leaflets and displays, all of which are an extension of the packaging itself. And they're the last chance your client has of reminding consumers of his product's promise.

Chapter 15

Amazing clients

Every account handler has clients or 'accounts' to work on. Your job is to look after them. You have a loyalty to your client. Advertising agencies depend wholly upon their clients. Managing them means attempting to build *their* business through advertising, and trying to increase *your* agency's client income. You have a loyalty to your agency too. You must ensure that the account is profitable, the invoices are dispatched promptly and, if your accounts department's efforts don't meet with success, make sure that clients pay up no later than when invoices are due.

Client management also means you must continually resolve conflicts between your client's wishes and the agency's point of view. You sometimes act as umpire. These conflicts can be more easily resolved by becoming a personal friend of the appropriate people in the client's organization.

However, no two advertisers are the same. Successfully handling advertising accounts is made all the more difficult by the tremendous variety of advertisers.

When they amaze you

Advertising clients can amaze you. Before going any further, I must make a few admissions.

Clients can be wonderful, and even inspiring. Most of them are under a great deal of pressure: a client's career is tied up with just one advertising account, whereas you are probably working on several. Clients tend to reserve their best face for dealing with their own colleagues. They won't let the people who pay their salaries be kept waiting. So *you* might not see them at their best.

In this respect, they're just like advertising agencies. I remember working with some agency people who thought themselves a lot more professional than their clients. After all, weren't their clients always changing their minds and blowing hot and cold? Well, the agency decided that it needed a new computer system to store prospects' names and data. So a couple of software companies were called in. We talked with them, but we didn't know what we really wanted in the way of software, and we certainly didn't know what systems might cost. We stumbled through a couple of these meetings and the software companies came back with some outline proposals. We weren't sure if they were what we wanted. So we talked some more, and then I think we gave up. These computer people would have been justified in cursing us as hopeless clients! It's difficult to be a good client.

Some of the worst advertising clients I've ever worked with have been in the property business. They often talk about advertising but seldom do it. On the other hand, I understand from friends in the property business that some of the worst clients they've ever worked with are advertising agencies. They often talk about moving but seldom do so! It's unsettling.

You've got to work with your clients whoever they are, and whatever kind of people they are. And advertising attracts some unusual people. Some agencies resign accounts that upset their staff too much. But virtually *every* advertising account causes some grief. Sometimes, there is only one solution and the client usually gets to it first. He fires the agency, but only after they've fallen out of love with one another. The separation occurs only after a period in which both sides lose enthusiasm for the relationship.

Anyway, here's some grief. A client once asked me which product he ought to promote next. I could only tell him that I had no idea. When he asked me why, I started trying to think why and said, 'You don't have a marketing strategy.' 'Yes I do,' he replied. 'What is it?' I asked. 'Well, I've got these products and I know what my sales targets are,' he pointed out. 'So you don't have a marketing strategy.' And he didn't. He was fired three weeks later.

Clients sometimes ask agencies to help them with their dirty work. One advertiser decided to fire one of his brand managers, but he could only implement his decision, he told the agency, once *it* had collected enough evidence. Thereafter the agency had to report every telephone conversation with the unfortunate manager and keep records of everything that happened on the account. The agency needed the client's income, so they kept the records and the guy was fired. From what I heard, he deserved to go, but what a painful process!

Client organizations can be quite complex, with lots of people involved in approving the advertising. Usually a number of people can turn down advertising, but only one person can buy it. The ideal is to present the agency's work to that one person. The trouble is that you often cannot even discuss the work with him. How can you deal with this sort of situation? A number of strategies are possible.

First, take every single person to whom you have to present the work seriously. Even if they don't have authority to buy the work, they could cause problems. Or they could make your path easier. They're probably tired of being towards the lower end of the hierarchy and working within a bureaucracy. You're a moment of fun. You're also the occasion when each individual's opinion is valued. Providing you listen, he probably won't mind being sold. But if you don't listen, he might mind a great deal. You've got a chance to be on his side in a way that his company cannot be. You are there to solve his problems.

A similar strategy can apply right down the line. Suppose you've struck up a good relationship with your day-to-day contact, and that your agency is producing good work which he always buys, but the advertising is getting vetoed further down the line by someone else. What should you do?

You must find out *why* it's being vetoed. However, this doesn't mean asking your contact for a list of his colleagues' reasons, as there may not be a reasonable answer. And you certainly don't want the guy who is vetoing your work to commit himself in writing on why he's turned it down. That would only entrench his position.

Nor do you want to meet him with your contact present. He's unlikely to change his mind in the presence of junior members of staff. In fact, he's more likely to use such a meeting to show his colleague who is really in charge, and he'll probably give you a hard time. You've got to meet him one to one. And then you listen to him.

At this stage you are not interested in having an argument. You are unlikely to win him round by a confrontation. You simply need to find out what his problems really are. And they could be anything – a detail, the proposition, the brief, the art direction. Or he might just be feeling neglected.

Once you've heard him out, there's no clear-cut rule on whether you go on defending the work. It really should hinge on whether or not you think he is right. It's unnecessary to state a point of view at the meeting itself, but there are some things to bear in mind in either case. You've got to respect his opinions. You should let him know that you appreciate his time and his views. You ought to let him know that you are going to think long and hard about them. And you probably will.

If in the end you don't take his advice, you had better be sure of your ground, and you had better be right. Then you go back to meet the same guy and let him know that you thought long and hard and so on . . . that you've considered the matter from every angle and that you're going to ask him to buy the work. At this stage you must explain the work's virtues in a form he'll appreciate. Then stop and await the response.

The most successful work I've ever handled was bought only after it had been turned down further up the line.

It may be that you think he was right to turn down your work. Or that he's made it very clear that if you bring back the same work he'll be very upset.

Even if, for some reason, he doesn't seem to be behaving like a professional, you've got to treat him as though he is. If you come back with a different campaign that takes account of what he said, make sure that he can see that is so. Don't let him think that you're still fighting for yesterday's campaign, even in your heart. Anyway, it would only upset him. That dispute is over and now you are working together. He's got to feel that you believe in the replacement work. Otherwise he might turn that down too.

Once you've heard out your client, he'll go one of two ways. Either he will be content to let things be, in which case you can probably win him as a friend just by being friendly to him. Or he will go on turning down your agency's work, in which case you've got problems and you are going to have to work hard to get right to the cause. (Maybe his best friend works at another agency and is after the account.)

Selling replacement work can be problematic. After a run of successes, a client of mine turned down a piece of work, then turned down our second effort and our third and our fourth. Two months later, he agreed to run our first recommendation. We'd both got into a rut and the resulting advertising wasn't very successful. The same strategy can apply right up the organization. Counter reason with reason, but counter hostility with friendship.

What can you do if you don't seem to be getting on with a client? I have a three-pronged solution. First, continue to be absolutely professional in all your work, however unprofessional you might feel your client is being. If he is behaving badly, make sure that your written records of decisions are especially thorough. Secondly, on no account resort to negative gossip, or moaning about him. It would just reinforce any problems. Thirdly, think positively about the account and your apparently 'difficult' client, and you'll be amazed how many problems will disappear. Account handlers exist to solve problems, not exacerbate them.

An affair of the pocket

When the late Bill Shankly, Liverpool Football Club's manager for many years, was asked whether football was for him a life and death business, he answered, 'No laddie, it's much more important than that'. So it is with clients. Clients are vital to advertising agencies, providing both income and work. Without clients, you have no agency.

Clients are probably your agency's sole source of income; very few agencies make money from, for example, selling research on to third parties. Without clients, your agency can't meet its payroll obligations. An agency's biggest clients typically account for 10–25 per cent of its revenue. The disappearance of a major client can mean staff redundancies.

Moreover, none of your agency's work, apart from self-promotion, can see the light of day unless it is approved by a client. The quality of any agency's work is heavily influenced by the kind of clients it has and, in the final analysis, an agency's work can be controlled by its clients. Some agencies excuse the work they are less than proud of by blaming it on the client: 'he wouldn't buy anything else'. Another school of thought holds that when it comes to buying good advertising, 'there is no such thing as a bad client', only agencies that produce or consent to run bad advertising.

Although advertising agencies need their clients, the clients don't need their agency. Most advertisers can find any number of agencies who will gladly handle their business – at virtually no notice. This is because advertising agencies head for advertising budgets as bees to honey. This imbalance can help to produce inconsiderate advertisers and overconsiderate agencies, opinionated clients and unopinionated agencies, and mediocre advertising. All, supposedly, to please the client.

The temptation is to give the advertiser what he wants, whether or not you believe it to be the best for him. It is so much easier to sell creative work that the advertiser already knows he wants, and any resistance within the agency can usually be quashed on the grounds that the client pays the bills. Indeed, some agencies operate on the principle that the client knows (advertising) best, and many are quite successful at building a business along these lines. Such agencies attract advertisers who want to stay in charge. But if things go wrong, and the advertising campaign doesn't work, the agency will be blamed anyway – and rightly so.

Others, who believe that, while a client knows his own business best, the agency should understand advertising best ask, 'Why pay a dog to bark and then bark yourself?' If you can't rely on your agency's judgement, is it the right agency for you? If you can rely on your advertising agency's judgement hold on to it.

On the other hand, agencies that have a point of view tend to attract advertisers who will rely on their agency's judgement, for at least as long as they are right. Their ideal kind of client might tend to say, 'We've taken our agency's advice so far, we'll take it now'. Triumphs will be shared, but the blame for any disasters will lie with the agency.

Service is very important. And in account handling, it's often the little things that count most. I had just taken over the management of a medium-sized account when the client called up. He wanted a reference of some fairly obscure advertising that had recently run in the United States. Within five minutes I was through to our contact at our sister agency in the USA. Within twenty minutes, copies of the advertisement were faxed to me in London, and fifteen minutes later they were with the client. Ten minutes on and my chief executive had come in to tell me how well I was running his new account. My client had called him up.

Service is simple. It's fairly easy to excel. As in many relationships, it's the little things that add up to success or separation.

But do you really like them?

Since clients matter more to agencies than agencies do to clients, it's up to you to get to know your clients really well. Close personal relationships can reinforce the business relationship. Nine times out of ten, the agency's account handler has to set about creating and maintaining them.

If there is poor personal chemistry between individuals at the client company and the agency, it's your problem to solve. Agencies are so much easier to fire. This means account handlers have to be good at getting on with all sorts of people, whether they are 'their kind of people' or not, and whatever their background.

Like the rest of humankind, advertisers like to be loved. Aim to be a friend of all your clients and they'll appreciate you. Even though you might not choose to go out drinking with your clients, you must do so. And when you aren't talking business, you'll spend most of your time either entertaining them or listening to them.

Over a period of time, you should aim to find out your client contact's background and career history, and as much about his personal circumstances as you can. You also want to establish how your contact fits into his company, who he reports to, when, and on what basis. And you'll need to meet those people too, and understand their motivations. Try to understand the chemistry of the relationships, and show sympathy wherever appropriate. Shared understanding of your client's circumstances is invaluable in a client/agency relationship.

You'll also aim to learn about your client contact's career ambitions and want to know who within the company is upwardly mobile, who isn't, and who is likely to move out. Try to discover your contact's personal prejudices about advertising – which campaigns and styles he likes, which he doesn't, and why.

Handling check

1 Are you taking enough interest in your clients?
2 Do you know them as people in their own right?
3 For example, do you know their personal circumstances and how they spend their time outside work?
4 Do you know their tastes, their likes and dislikes?
5 Who do the people you deal with report to within their own organization, how and on what?

6   Do you know what they are looking for from your contact?
7   And what do they expect of the agency?
8   What are the internal politics of your client's organization?
9   Do you know who is upwardly mobile, who isn't and who is likely to move out?
10   And do you know the individuals' personal prejudices about advertising?
11   How they like meetings to be run and how they like to be sold?

What really matters to your client?

Handling makes the advertising business go round. Some clients can be taken in up to a point. It seems that they believe their agency is producing good work, even when it's not. Clients tend to believe in their agency's ability to produce good advertising. If they didn't, they would fire it. However, some agencies are much better than others for particular kinds of work. And some are simply in-effective, but their clients don't know it.

So from the client's point of view, advertising ability is not something that's always taken into account in valuing an agency/client relationship. It's taken for granted. What actually matters are all the other things. And they almost all concern handling. Have you found out the best way to work with each client? How they like to be handled is critical. If they can't enjoy working with their advertising agency, who can they enjoy working with?

Few advertising accounts are lost through poor planning, or poor creative or media work. Few clients turn around and say, 'They took us up the wrong creative route, so we fired them'. Or 'They're just not up to it from a media point of view. They had to go'. Or 'Their advertising wasn't up to it. It's as simple as that'. True, it would be uncharitable for departing clients to loose off in public like that, but I believe they don't even think such thoughts.

Sometimes, a fall in sales leads – often mistakenly – to a review of the advertising campaign, which in turn leads to a switch of agency. And some agencies resign accounts if the agency thinks the client is going in the wrong direction. But overwhelmingly it's much simpler than that.

Clients and agencies leave one another because they lose enthusiasm for the relationship. And, after a while, the client starts fooling around. The quality of most client/agency relationships deteriorates significantly for six months to a year *before* the break is made. And over most of that time, the relationship could be saved by either party if they made a big enough effort. So it's down to you, the account handler, to hold on to the business.

Find out what increases your client's enthusiasm and what reduces it. What makes him excited and what doesn't. And respond. It's normally the little things that upset clients most: late for meetings, late work and late invoices; wrong contact reports, inaccurate work, and invoices that surprise them. And account handlers who don't listen. Why should they put up with incompetence on the little things when they pay your agency so much money? Who needs bad account handling? Clients want to feel proud of their agencies. And it's quite difficult to feel proud of an incompetent agency.

However, like all other human beings, clients most of all really want to be loved. Which means giving the highest and the truest within you.

Chapter 16

How to use the agency systems

The natural state of an advertising agency is chaos. Without proper systems, the life of an account handler can be confusing, traumatic and short. And systems need to be administered if they are to work. From time to time advertising's spontaneous and pressured people have to be kept gently in line, which is largely the account handler's job. Unfortunately, many account handlers are weak on administration and gain a reputation for unreliability and 'account fumbling'. Your oversights have a habit of catching up with you.

In fact, the best account handlers don't seem to spend much time on administration and systems. They use them to their advantage and don't make mistakes. They get their work done efficiently and have fewer problems than the average account handler.

The more systematically you approach your work, the more you will achieve. And you'll have a slightly less frustrating life. You can rely upon a good system. And in most agencies there are at least three. They concern approvals, buying and invoicing.

1. Quality control

Let's start with approval systems. They're managed by your traffic department, whose job it is to reconcile account handlers' demands with the agency's limited resources and to ensure an orderly flow of work through the agency. They also help implement quality control systems.

They are therefore concerned with questions like: can the agency deliver what you've requested? And what's the best way to do so? You need to get them on your side if you want to get your own work through. The best way to do this is to listen to their advice, and to agree each course of action with them, before you embark upon it.

Traffic should have a pretty good idea of how busy each creative team is at any one time. They'll know how many jobs they've got on and when they're due. You should keep them posted of your likely requirements.

Try not to spring surprises. They'll be able to advise you on what you can promise your client, if you speak to them first. You should also let them know as soon as you have definite requirements. Once you've agreed with your client that, say, you'll put a brief in next week you can let traffic know. They'll appreciate the warning.

Once you or your planner have constructed a brief, you'll need to get it approved. While some agencies don't have approval systems and some don't have traffic departments, most have both. Usually, traffic will put the brief under the nose of the people who have to sign it off or turn it down. So you give your brief to traffic. They circulate it and return it to you with or without comments – approved or rejected.

Traffic are particularly concerned with some aspects of your brief. And with good reason.

Timing: bearing in mind the other jobs that the allotted creative team have in hand, have you allowed enough time for them to do the work? This can throw up difficult issues. The account may have been the prerogative of one particular creative team who are now busy on other work, or on holiday. Choice of creative team becomes an issue if timing is a problem. Who else is available?

Production budget: they'll want to know whether you've specified a production budget. And whether it's likely to be enough to do the job.

Production timing: they'll also look ahead to any scheduled media appearances and any you are likely to spring on them. They'll be concerned as to whether there are air dates, or press copy dates, for the advertising to be produced. Often, there aren't.

But if you satisfy them on these points and have approvals from the powers that be, traffic will allow your brief into creative, on the agreed terms. These agreed terms are now the fixed reference point for all concerned with the job. They shouldn't be changed without another brief to which everyone agrees.

Traffic should also help your creative team by refusing, on their behalf, additional work which would prevent the team from delivering your work. But this system only works if the agency is committed to your brief in the first place. Without its commitment, your brief is likely to sink. Especially if you are in an under-resourced agency. That's why the *system* is important.

Traffic should help you further. They'll monitor your creative team's progress especially as they approach the agreed internal review date, when their work is discussed within the agency. Traffic will ensure that each creative team are aware of the jobs they have on and when they are supposed to complete them. This is handy support. And they'll get the team's work through its approval process. The minimum is usually the agency's creative director, but the planner and account director are usually also involved. The significance of this system is two-fold.

First, experienced advertising people (and some less experienced ones) are more likely than not to spot a duff advertisement, which saves you the embarrassing task of presenting it to your client. They're also more likely to be able to spot a winner and make sure it runs. There may be times when you feel that a complex approval process is a nuisance. Especially if the work is due, you are itching to get into a cab to see the client, and you can't find your creative director. But it does have advantages.

Secondly, it means that the work you present is supported by your agency. It isn't only one creative team's response to the brief. Because it has been approved, it's got the backing of the agency, and this should reassure your client too. It also means that your senior colleagues have to commit themselves. So, on the one hand, you get the benefit of their judgements when you need it and, on the other, they don't have any come-backs against you later on. If the client turns down work that you present, they could only agree with the client if they admit that they've changed their minds.

These approval processes apply at the first creative stage and, usually in a more diluted form, at the second stage. For example, a concept for a press advertisement might require approval by the agency's managing director and creative director, but the sub-sequent copy might only need to be approved by the account director and creative group head. (In some big agencies, creative teams are organized into groups of teams, each of which has its own chief, called a creative group head.)

The subsequent setting proof of the advertisement might need the account manager, the copywriter and art director to sign it off, while the colour proof from each publication which needs checking mainly for colour reproduction will need special checking by an expert. Incidentally, it's important that the creative team who produced the work maintain quality control of the finished product. They have the best idea of how it ought to look and they care as much as anyone about the final advertisement's appearance.

2. Buying to order

You need buying systems too. If you can't control who is spending what on your accounts, you're likely to get into difficulty.

In theory, no-one from art directors to production should spend your client's money without your approval. Two things ought to happen first. They should tell you what they want to do and how much it will cost. You should then get your client's explicit authority (or know that he'll be happy about paying the cost). Normally, that means providing a written estimate to your client, but if you need immediate approval you must simply call him.

On most production jobs you'll provide an estimate at the beginning of the job for approval. However, it's in the nature of the production process that the job needs extra work done at some stage. Perhaps you need more editing time on a film, or to retouch a photograph, or to change some copy, to get the right line breaks. If you haven't allowed enough for corrections, you should get your client's authority. On no account should you let your colleagues spend money that may not be available.

Once you've got the approval, the work can be set in motion. Authority is normally given to suppliers on a written form called an 'art order' or 'buying instruction'. And your suppliers should append a copy of that order to their invoice.

3. Job bags

There's also a system to ensure that clients get invoiced for all they owe. It revolves around job bags. All estimates, buying orders and invoices are filed in a job bag. And there's one file or bag for the production of each advertisement or job. A job bag is opened every time you issue a creative brief. And a copy of the brief is kept in the bag too.

In most agencies, the traffic department will keep the file up to date until the job is finished, at which point the job bag is closed and passed to accounts. Your accounts people will draw up an invoice for your approval. If you're unlucky you might have to draft it yourself. Then the agency can start making money.

Chapter 17

Managing money and politics

Considering their high quality of personnel, it could be argued that most advertising agencies are fairly badly run. Handling the business is more exciting than managing the agency.

But account handlers are day-to-day managers of the business that their clients provide. Account handlers should ensure that their accounts do their agency good, as well as helping the advertiser. Account handlers also tend to end up running the advertising agency, if they don't leave the advertising business first, or become a client. So why are many account handlers relatively poor business managers?

On the whole, they're simply not motivated by management: it doesn't provide them with the same buzz. Yes, they want to be successful and they'll work flat out when it's necessary. But they probably don't recognize a connection between good business habits and success – with less effort expended. So *there's* an opportunity.

The root of all prosperity

Advertising agencies vary in their pricing and credit policies, and hence in the income they receive from similarly sized accounts as well as the timing of its arrival.

Agencies have traditionally passed on only 85 per cent of their advertisers' expenditure to the media, retaining 15 per cent for themselves. They usually apply a similar formula to research and production, marking up their suppliers' invoices by 17.65 per cent, so taking 15 per cent of the gross amount that's invoiced to the client. Some agencies will charge the clients just as much as they can get away with, while maintaining the pretence of the mark-up. But by and large an agency expects to earn £150,000 income for every £1,000,000 their clients spend on advertising.

Agencies don't always make 15 per cent on media. The commission level itself can vary. Agencies can charge their clients a fee on top of commission, to reach the remuneration level they think appropriate for the work required. Or they will negotiate a fee instead of commission. This can be based on the projected advertising expenditure, whether or not that *final* spend materializes.

So, for example, a client who plans to spend £1 million a year on advertising might agree to pay his agency £150,000 in twelve monthly instalments of £12,500. In return, the agency would rebate the media commission. This arrangement produces an even flow of income to the agency. Depending on the detail of the deal, it can fix the agency's income at this level, whatever the subsequent spend. A high spending advertiser who needs relatively little creative work might seek to pay less than 15 per cent commission, and have the remainder rebated to him.

Fees are also charged for non-commissionable (below-the-line) work like sales support and point-of-sale material, product brochures and direct mail packages.

Agencies tend to invoice clients for 50 per cent of their production costs once the estimate for each job is approved by the client and before production starts. The remaining 50 per cent is payable on completion of the job. They pay the media at about the time their clients pay them, although some agencies are notoriously slow at invoicing their clients and paying their suppliers.

Whatever formula applies, each account-handling team should be able to project the income they expect each of their advertising accounts to generate. Even if they can't say when it is likely to occur.

Agencies also vary in the extent to which they charge incidental costs back to the client. Such costs can include everything from lunching the advertiser to the cost of buying his trade newspapers, from slides for presentations to out-of-house copywriting charges, And, of course, the cost of motorbikes to carry urgent items to and fro. Some agencies bundle many of these costs together monthly, and invoice each client accordingly. Others build them into production bills, specifying some items, but hiding others. Many incidental items are never recharged, especially to high spending advertisers who provide a correspondingly high income to their agency.

The more such costs are recharged, the lower are an agency's overheads, and the higher its profits. At least, in the short term. In the longer run, it could get a reputation for being unjustifiably expensive.

However, invoices issued don't equal money in the bank. Many advertisers require prompting before they pay. The agency's accounts department may need support from the account handler in chasing the agency's invoices due, if the client's accounts department haven't been authorized to pay. An agency can make or lose money simply through the timing of its payments to suppliers and receipt of its clients' cheques.

The account director is usually responsible for pricing the agency's services. Together with the account handling team, he must take a view on how much time the agency must commit to each advertiser. Agency personnel usually have their own charge-out rate, expressed in £ per hour, which reflects the value of their contribution to the agency's work. By estimating the total number of hours each relevant agency employee is likely to have to spend, it's possible to arrive at an estimate of the agency's total time costs. This can be set against the income expected from the account.

And, of course, agencies exist to make profits. Typically, they might make only 1–2 per cent of their client's total advertising expenditure, but this roughly equates to 5–20 per cent of income after media and outside suppliers are paid.

So how can a client be made more profitable? The best way to get more income from a client is to find an advertising solution that works so well that it justifies an increased advertising expenditure, and hence more income for the agency. Effective campaigns can help advertiser and agency alike.

Even in the absence of a higher expenditure, a good advertising solution can turn an unprofitable account around by reducing the amount of time the agency has to spend on further creative and media work. Effective advertising frees up agency resources to produce more work for other income-generating clients.

The agency might find new advertising opportunities for its clients, for example, other audiences to reach with the advertising's message, which justify additional media expenditure. Or new products to promote.

The agency could propose undertaking extra research for the client and charge for its services. Or it could try to expand below-the-line into print and design.

If an account threatens to remain unprofitable, the agency might simply propose to put its prices up. It could charge additional fees to make up the gap between expected income and a satisfactory level of profit, or invoice for actual hours spent but not paid for on the existing terms.

In fact, the agency might be happy to take a loss on an account. The agency might need the business at any price, as a spur to growth, an aid to morale or a boost to its prestige. It might be a charity account, or the account might simply be set for more growth, and hence income for the agency. A loss-making account could be worth hanging on to.

Handling check

1   How much income do you expect from each client?
2   When should the relevant invoices be issued?
3   When will the agency have to do the relevant work?
4   What are the implications for cash-flow?
5   How many hours would the projected income from each client keep the agency team on the client's business?
6   How much time will the work take?
7   Should you be doing as much work for this amount of income?
8   Should you be charging more for the agency's time?
9   How can you generate more business and income from each account?

How Much Will All This Cost?

You are responsible for ensuring that the agency makes money from your accounts. And simply making some income isn't enough. You need to do so profitably.

That means making more money than it costs to service a particular account. An advertising agency's biggest cost is people. A good rule of thumb is that you cost your agency about two to three times what you are actually paid once you take into account secretarial support, national insurance and rates, telephones and other overheads – not to mention the accounts department itself.

So if your account ties up one account handler and 50 per cent of each of a copywriter and an art director, a media planner and a media buyer, a traffic handler and a production specialist, then at an average salary of, say, £20,000 the salary cost to date is £80,000. Add some board-level involvement and you are up to £100,000. Multiply by a factor of 2–3 and you can see that your agency needs an income of between £200,000 and £300,000 to service your business, depending on its overheads. And it needs to make profits too. Your account might be costing the agency a great deal of money!

More and more often advertising agencies have their employees record the time they spend, so that they can more precisely analyse each account's profitability. However, these records are often filled in inaccurately, some time after the event, particularly by the creative people who are often the most expensive in terms of time. And many agencies are reluctant to ask their clients for more money.

If you find that you are undercharging, and you ask for more money, you could find yourself in great difficulty. Your client might argue that you have agreed to the existing arrangements – whether or not you agreed that they could be reviewed – so why change them now? He might feel that you are taking a short-term view of the relationship in seeking more money now – even if he could fire you before tomorrow's jam becomes available. He might say that your persistence is causing him to look at the account in a different way – the veiled threat.

Equally, agencies get upset when clients try to reduce the agency's income, say, halfway through a campaign. Many agencies take a long-term view of client income on the grounds that today's small account may be tomorrow's big account. And although they might make a loss creating a particular campaign, once it's up it should run and run, producing lots of income for the agency. On this approach, the best way to make money is to produce outstanding campaigns which go on running, with only modest revisions year after year. While the agency keeps on picking up its 15 per cent.

But the trouble with the long term is that it might never arrive. In the short term, some profitable accounts are subsidizing other unprofitable accounts. And why should they? If you review short-term profitability, say on a monthly basis, at least you can see what sort of assumptions you are making about the pattern of workload and future income.

Ideally, you need to establish a sensible way of charging at the outset. And agree when, and on what basis, negotiations will occur. And there are lots of ways to charge.

A question of attitude

Account handlers should be happy. But a lot of the time they are worried or depressed, or both. Of course, it's difficult to be happy in an unhappy agency. But account handlers influence the climate in which they work more than anyone else. As an account handler you are in the firing line and you work with all the agency's departments. You can spread gloom or happiness quite quickly.

The best course is to redouble your efforts when the chips are down. Keep cool when all around you are losing their heads. And make every effort to enjoy your work. Most agencies are short on people who have these kind of qualities. They could do with a few more. You could be one of them. In fact, gloomy account handlers are a luxury few agencies can afford. So effervesce, however quietly. Moreover, this helps to get everyone else motivated.

Equally, if account handlers don't believe in their agency's values and its future, it's likely that no-one else will, starting with your clients. And there's no point in being rebellious. Everyone has their limitations, you and me included. Don't get upset at other people's weaknesses, even when they're your boss's. They are his problem. And while you *may* be able to help, your main job is to work out your own.

So always endeavour to believe in your agency's key staff. How will you measure up when you run your own agency? There are always lessons to be learned. If you can't get on, get out. You're in the firing line, remember.

Handling check

1   Do you feel happy about your agency?
2   Are you motivated and excited by your work?

3 Do you believe in the agency's future? (Do you know where it's going?)
4 Do you believe in its philosophy? (Do you know what that is? Has your agency got one?)
5 Do you believe in its key staff?

7 Ways to survive agency politics

Some agencies are ruled by fear. Like most organizations, advertising agencies can be political places. Not, of course, in the party political sense, but through each individual's objectives with regard to personal projects and career development and the way they go about achieving them. While empire-building for the agency as a whole is usually beneficial, this principle shouldn't be applied selectively.

Agencies have more than their fair share of oversized egos which can be ultra-sensitive to criticism. Account handlers often find themselves up against them. Especially when you try to bring the agency's service departments into line with the client's objectives, or reconcile the client to the agency's position. How can you survive advertising agency politics?

The best strategy is not to play. This usually means trying to get on with everyone and avoiding politics wherever possible. Don't tie your colours to anyone's mast. They might be the loser.

1. Wherever possible, avoid arguments. Don't go beyond stating your opinion. Why? Whenever you lose an argument you risk losing face, but whenever you win an argument at someone's expense, you lose a friend. You lose either way.

2. Listen to what other people say and avoid being dogmatic. Everybody in agencies likes being listened to, and none like pat answers. Then simply speak the truth as you see it.

3. Ask others to excel and expect the best of them. Try to build their self-confidence, and compliment them on their performance whenever you rightly can. Bear malice towards no-one.

4. Avoid being overcritical of others' work. Most agency egos are hyper-sensitive. 'That's a good start towards a solution' is more constructive than 'That's weak'. Whenever possible, preface a criticism with a compliment. It's much less likely to be resented. Be careful how you do it.

5. Avoid being critical of other people, except your own staff,

whom you lead by example. Always try to resist the temptation to criticize others behind their backs. For their part, they may gossip about you, and such words have a way of getting reported back. How you talk about colleagues may say more about you than about them.

6. Try to think things through from your colleagues' point of view. If something you've done upsets someone, work out why, not why you think you're right. Put yourself second, and you'll come out on top.

7. Be a good company man! Your agency should win through in the end. If you really don't think you can help, this could be a good time to leave.

If you can be known for the unbiased truth of your opinions and the strength of your judgement, you are a long way towards achieving the respect that good account handlers need. It's up to you.

Handling check

1   Are you playing agency politics? Why?
2   Are you being dogmatic or arguing with your colleagues?
3   Do you listen to your colleagues' opinions?
4   Do you believe in your colleagues? (And believe in yourself?)
5   Are you critical of them? In what way?
6   Can you see things from their point of view?
7   Do you put the agency first?

One more thing. If you are perplexed, set aside the reasoning mind. Think positively and kindly, and you may be surprised to find your problems solved!

10 ways to help improve your agency

Every agency has weaknesses and many of them are shared in common. Consider whether your agency passes these ten tests.

1. Is your agency goal-orientated? Do you know what its goals are? Do your colleagues?

2. Does it have a strategy to realize its goals?

3. Do the staff take responsibility for their own areas of work? And are they accountable to one another, or do they spend time meddling in one another's areas of work?

4. Is your agency managed, or do you simply rely on crisis management? To some people, managing means just muddling through.

5. Do you all say what you mean, and mean what you say, to the people you ought to say it to? Or do you say it to other people?

6. Do your colleagues moan about the agency? Do you guide and develop and inspire them? Or do you join in the moaning?

7. Does your agency have a disciplined approach to details like internal meetings? Do they start on time?

8. Do your colleagues play politics? It's amazing what can be achieved if everyone works together instead.

9. Do you spend time gossiping about one another?

10. Have you decided to succeed, come what may?

Chapter 18

How to handle meetings

Filling in Time

Client meetings are critical to successful account handling. You must be on your toes on every such occasion. You are trying to create and develop a special kind of chemistry as well as achieve the goals of each particular meeting. It's your chance to shine, or to embarrass yourself and the agency. To be successful, each meeting requires careful handling beforehand, during it and afterwards.

Your first decision is whether to have a meeting at all. In some agencies client meetings are a substitute for getting on with the work itself. Either the account team are too busy meeting the client to produce the work, or they feel they can't produce much in the way of work, so they decide to major on meetings – to keep the client happy.

An account handler once told a new client about his system of meetings. He explained that there would be progress meetings within the agency each week in which the account handler would participate, and weekly meetings with the client to review how things were going. There would be monthly meetings with the client to see how much progress had been made in the month as a whole, mini quarterly reviews and big six-monthly reviews involving the client's colleagues. His monologue had extended to about five minutes and left the client and me a bit dazed when I suddenly got a chance to interject. 'In other words', I said with great emphasis, 'We'll have meetings when we need them.' End of subject.

In fact, your clients should look forward to agency meetings. They are their chance to escape from their corporate environment. And you can help them to enjoy each meeting. But you should be careful not to have too many of them.

Once you've decided to have a meeting, you need to decide who should attend and when it should be held. Will you have the work ready by that time? Often, you can't get the people you need when you want them. And you might need to fix an internal agency get-together a day or so before the client meeting in order to go over the subject matter together and agree on what you are trying to achieve.

Get Prepared

For clients, meetings with the agency are often an event. They look forward to being entertained and sold. They shouldn't be disappointed.

For account handlers, meetings can be an ordeal, especially if you are underprepared. Hours of agency work are invested in the outcome of most meetings. And if the meeting is unsuccessful, there is always the risk that the agency will have to do the work over again.

As it's mainly through meetings that the client meets the agency, it's worth being well prepared beforehand. Here are some of the things you'll need.

A checklist for client meetings

1. Agenda
2. Contact report (i.e. minutes of last meetings) and/or status report (regular progress statement)
3. Relevant creative and media briefs, advertising concepts, copy, storyboards (a sequence of roughs of key stills for a proposed commercial, usually put together on one board), proofs
4. Media schedules
5. Production schedules, budgets, estimates, quotes and recent invoices

6. Relevant research and agency documents, background data, competitive advertising and support material

7. Business cards, agency brochures, pencils, pads, tea, coffee, water.

Meetings can go wrong even before they start. Recently, an account director had to organize a meeting and start by picking up two new business prospects in reception and getting me out of another meeting. Ten minutes after my colleague's meeting was due to start, I was still in the first meeting and so left it anyway to find out what was going on.

The account director assured me that we hadn't heard from our guests and suggested that the rain had defeated their efforts to visit us. Feeling uneasy, I called reception. As soon as I announced myself, there was a fair amount of shouting in reception as the receptionist dropped the receiver. She had gone chasing after our two prospects who had *left* the building moments before, after waiting 25 minutes for us. They had arrived early and asked for me. Our temporary receptionist had dialled the wrong number, asked for me and been misheard by someone who declared that Nigel (another Nigel) was out to lunch with his secretary.

For our part, we hadn't informed reception that we expected prospects, nor checked immediately they were late. Needless to say, it was a very difficult meeting. The next day, I decided to wait in reception for the next prospect.

Handling check

1 Have you made sure you've got everything you need for the meeting (e.g. media and production schedules and quotes, concepts and copy, past and competitive advertisements, invoices and budgets)?

2 And will the people you *need* be there? Are you presenting to the people who can say 'yes' to your proposals or is this simply a preparatory meeting?

3 Does the client know what you want him to bring (e.g. briefs, research, below-the-line support, product details)? Will a reminding note help?

4 Do you know exactly what you want the meeting to achieve? Do your colleagues know? What does the client want out of the meeting?

5 Which relevant papers should you send ahead? (Never send

creative work, but if you want the client's considered view on some *thinking*, you'll have to give him time to consider it before the meeting.)

6 What is the best agenda for the meeting?
7 Have you decided how you want to handle the meeting? What is most likely to go wrong? How would you handle that?
8 What is the client going to want to talk about? What is he likely to ask you about? (Do you have the answers?)
9 Can you be ready half an hour before the meeting is due to start? Why not? (It gives you time to think and to cope with any last-minute problems.)
10 Is the meeting room booked and set up?
11 Is the agency's work finished?
12 Are your people ready?
13 Have you tipped off reception to expect your guests?

Decisions, decisions

Advertising meetings are mainly about people management. You set the tone for each client meeting in the first few seconds. When the client meets you he automatically assesses your mood and your feelings towards him.

Rather than try to do the same, an account handler's best strategy is to ensure that he is creating the right environment. In my experience this goes beyond what you say or even how you say it, and a lot deeper than 'non-verbal communication' or 'body language'. It gets right down to what you think.

If you are trying to look composed but really you are very worried, or if you are trying to behave as though you respect the client but really you don't, it's going to show through sooner or later. And your client can pick this up at the very beginning of any meeting. So what's the solution to this sort of problem? Rather than *pretend* to be composed, it's better to be composed. If necessary, give yourself an extra five minutes before each meeting to get composed. And rather than *pretend* to respect your client, respect him. Respect costs nothing.

Once you've allowed your client to take a reading of your feelings, his barriers can start to come down. And you can begin to establish how he feels. His mood can tell you how to handle the meeting.

If it looks as though he's got something up his sleeve, you're probably better off finding out what it is before you launch into a sales pitch. And if he looks upset, you'd better find out why. There may be no point in trying to sell anything if he's upset with the agency. The best you can hope for is an inconclusive result. A good way to explore these possibilities is simply to ask your client what's going on at his place, how things are going, and so on. You might pick up all sorts of information. If you can ask after your client's family, by name, you are doing even better! You are that bit more likely to have a successful meeting.

Then you can start off by explaining just what you want to cover in the meeting, and allowing your client to confirm that he's happy with that agenda, or to add extra times or query your plan at the outset.

Know the meeting's objective. If you are there to take a brief, don't start selling the agency. And don't start discussing possible creative solutions. They aren't your job and anyway they come later, once you've agreed on the brief and passed it to your creative team.

Once you've got these items out of the way you can start selling, if the plan is to sell some of the agency's work. This usually involves starting out by confirming your client's needs (the assumptions you have made) before going on to show how your solution fulfils those needs. It's not simply a matter of showing him your work.

You'll need to stop selling in order to allow the client to buy your work or to voice his objections. You need to consider whether each objection affects your work and if so how, or whether it simply needs handling. (Chapter 10 on selling creative work goes into all of this in more detail.)

You should also remember what your client says. It enables you to develop a clear picture of his thinking which is vital for account development.

Client meetings can involve redundant discussion. It's much better to 'waste' time at the beginning of the meeting when you are checking your client out, or at the end of a meeting when you can allow him to unwind.

The best way I know of to take charge of an undisciplined meeting is as follows:

1. Allow everyone else to have a say.
2. Pick out all the relevant points in a summary statement of your own.

3. Then state the conclusion, if one has been reached, or the issue if it remains outstanding.

4. If you really have got to a conclusion but everyone wants to go on talking, you might be advised to say, 'That just leaves us with the issue of timing . . .' or any other minor issue.

Meetings get unruly when people don't listen to one another. So make sure you listen. Similarly, if you think a decision has been made, it's usually best to state it. This avoids the problem of people subsequently disagreeing about what was decided when they get your contact report.

Handling check

1 Do you welcome clients with warmth and enthusiasm? (The tone for the meeting is often determined in the first few seconds of contact.)
2 Have you assessed their mood? (What does that tell you about how you have to handle the meeting?)
3 Does something seem to be on their minds? (If so, you had better let them unburden themselves, rather than have them spring it on you later.)
4 Have you asked them what's new? (It often brings things to light.) And have you continued to show interest in their work and personal circumstances? (You should try to be their friend.)
5 Are you going to listen? (You can develop your view while the client is talking.)
6 Are you going to sell? (Will you know when to stop selling?)
7 Can you keep assessing what your client thinks and how you can develop his views?
8 Do you notice when the discussion wanders off what you are trying to decide on? (Can you bring it back?)
9 Can you summarize what has been agreed?

The follow-through

After each meeting, it's important to produce a short written note clearly showing each decision. It'll save you time and allow your colleagues to see how the account is developing. It also acts as a confirmation of each decision.

It's also important to produce it quickly. If you can, set aside time after each meeting to produce the report. And get it distributed within an hour.

Since your colleagues will usually be keen to find out how the meeting has gone, you might want to drop by their offices right away. If the meeting has been a success, you should drop by and thank your colleagues (for the work they have done). Even congratulate them.

If you've got bad news, it's often best to tell the people who are involved straightaway rather than allow them to hear through the grapevine. However, if you've encountered problems but believe that the situation is still retrievable it might be premature to spread gloom.

Of course, if a meeting has gone badly, you had really better work out why it did so. Was it the work or the way you handled it? It's often appropriate to call your client the day after a meeting and tease out of him how he feels about it.

If the client bought your work you might congratulate him on doing so. On no account should you ask him if he still likes the work, as this gives him an opportunity to change his mind.

If there were things you promised to get moving on immediately, let him know what you've already achieved. If he undertook to do certain things you might remind him of his commitments by thanking him for agreeing to do them.

Handling check

1   Do you produce a short written note of what was decided and especially who is going to do what?
2   Can you let them know (virtually) immediately? (A written contact report should often be supplemented by a personal discussion.)
3   And can they confirm that they will do it?
4   Have you passed on any good news and handed out the congratulations?
5   And personally told the people involved of any bad news? (It's worse for them to hear it on the grapevine.)
6   And agreed on why?
7   And either way, have you thanked the team and do they feel sufficiently motivated? (Do you?)
8   Have you checked out how the client feels in retrospect?
9   Does he know of further progress you are making?

Chapter 19

Winning more business

Advertising agencies are products too. And most agencies, like most products, need to be *sold*. Some of them even run advertisements for themselves.

New business is advertising agencies' lifeblood. It enables you to hire staff (more than you fire) and to replace decaying and departing business. Mostly, account handlers have to make the running for new business. Moreover, most agency personnel enjoy the excitement of new business. It's a perk. If you aren't chasing new business you'll lose most of your dynamic people. They *need* to be chasing new business at least some of the time. Let them. Encourage them. Channel their energies. New business comes in two forms – from existing clients who agree to spend more on advertising, and from new clients.

Typically, winning new business from new clients necessitates getting considered by the advertiser, getting on his shortlist, and winning the resulting competition or pitch.

An advertising agency's new business plan must reflect its future income projection. However, most advertising agencies don't have much of a new business plan. If you ask them what they are doing to bring in business you may find their situation is more chaotic than that of their worst clients. Some are able to rely on their reputation, while others simply keep their ears close to the ground.

What's your new business plan?

What should your agency's new business programme include? It should fit your future goals concerning the rate of growth, the type of business you want by sector, the size of account you want, and the kind of advertising you want to produce. While one agency may be determined to double its income within two years, another may want to replace any business it loses. It may be more concerned with the quality of its work, or the quiet life!

Let's start at the money end of the equation. Your agency's income forecast is made up of the money you expect from current clients, together with the income you plan to get from new clients which you haven't yet acquired. And it is upon the forecast that the agency makes its business decisions: how many people to employ, how much to pay them and so on. So once a new business target is set, it needs to be realized.

New business goals can be spelt out in financial terms, e.g. a £1 million per annum client to come on-stream in May and a £3 million per annum client in September (together producing £200,000 income for the agency before the end of the year, given an even flow of spend, and £600,000 income in the following 12 months). This might seem unrealistic. How can you know what is going to come your way? All I can say is that the more specific you are about your objectives, the more likely you are to achieve them.

With so many advertisers around, and so many agencies after their business, how can you decide where you will try to get your new business? You can make a priority of a particular business sector, or size of advertising budget, or try to develop a reputation for excelling at particular kinds of advertising solution. In fact, you can focus in any way you choose.

Business breeds business. Agencies tend to get more campaign opportunities resembling the last one they did well. You'll attract advertisers who appreciate your experience and like your style.

By how much does your agency plan to grow next year? And in the following years?

Handling check

1 Are you trying to get new business?
2 What are you actually doing to get it?
3 Have you made a list of the kinds of business you want to work for by their business area?

4   And what kinds of client (top of the market or growing, good advertising clients, or big budgets)?
5   And have you found out who the decision makers are in each of these firms? (Do you know who influences their decisions? There will *always* be someone who will reinforce the decision. Find out who it is.)
6   And made contact with them?
7   And do you know what they want from an advertising agency? (Have you talked to them?)
8   Have you decided which kinds of need you want to satisfy?
9   And what your agency's philosophy is?
10   And why any client should come to your agency?
11   What are your business objectives? (See the early chapters of this book and treat yourself as the client.)

How to cultivate contacts

It's not a matter of 'who you know', it's more a case of who knows you, and especially of those who judge you to be good, that helps get new business opportunities. Personal contacts don't usually provide you with new business on a plate. But they can get you on to a long list of agencies considered for the business, or give you a chance to argue that you should be there. This isn't surprising. The advertising world revolves around people, and from the advertiser's point of view, dealing with someone they know and appreciate is always an advantage. They can be fairly sure that they won't be let down.

Given that advertising agencies work for all sorts of people in all kinds of business, how do you make contacts? You might well have started your advertising career without any contacts in positions of influence. As most of the people who started out when you did will also develop their own careers, you should keep in touch with them even though it may be as much as ten years before these contacts pay off. But you can enjoy them in the meantime.

Almost all the people you work with, in your agency, at advertisers and in the media, are worth keeping in view. And you should keep within *their* field of vision – discreetly. Of course, you have to have made a favourable impression and done a good job before these people pay off in the future. That is the beauty of contacts. Contacts are only worth anything to you if you're worth something to them. There's no such thing as a free contact.

Opportunities to make contacts occur often – at parties, dinners, lunches, and so on. You have to make a point of finding out what people do, what their goals are, and so on. Friends of friends provide yet more opportunities. And just one new contact a month makes 60 in five years!

But contacts require servicing. They can be developed or lost. Development usually takes a great deal of time and effort, and you may have to persist for many years. In fact, it should become part of your way of doing business, and stay with you throughout your career.

Let's start with the basics. While your business card should always be handy, you are unlikely to get far by handing it out in an unsolicited way. However brilliant your conversation, the card is unlikely to motivate your new contact to call you.

You need a reference so that you can call or write to them. On the whole, this shouldn't be done without a pretext, but there are many ways to create one. If someone asks about your agency or your work, an offer to send your agency's brochure, leaflet, case history or simply some advertisements will almost always be accepted. So you'll get their details.

If you don't follow the contact up, it burns out quickly. You should follow it up with a brief covering letter, either reminding them that you are attaching the promised item and thanking them for their interest, or expressing more interest in their work, and promising to keep in touch or suggesting a fresh meeting some time ahead. Then your contact is started.

Such contacts have to be carefully nurtured in order to blossom and grow. You must stay in touch and keep interested in them without being too pushy. You'll need to use the phone.

New brochures, reports, campaigns, Christmas cards, articles interesting to your contact and any press coverage on the agency all provide opportunities for renewing contact. So can important changes in your own life. You don't need to indulge in complicated covering letters: short notes, or even signed one-liners on a compliments slip make your point, take less of your time to write and less of your contact's time to read. You must also keep track of what your contacts are up to – you have to make the effort to be interested in them. Generally speaking, a handful of assorted letters, calls and cards keep a contact warm.

The best thing is continually to keep in mind what you can do for other people. The more you can help them, the more likely they are to find a way to help you. Give first, collect later.

Speculative schizophrenia

Suppose you've just been invited to pitch. What do you do next?

First, you find out why you've been shortlisted. You need to know why your agency is in demand. It'll also give you an idea of what the prospective client already knows about your agency.

Secondly, find out who else they've shortlisted. If they've chosen three different kinds of agency, then they haven't decided what *kind* of agency they need. That could be an aspect of the pitch. If they've chosen three agencies all like one another, then they know what they're looking for.

Thirdly, make a preliminary decision as to whether you want to pitch for the business. And let the prospect know.

Fourthly, start to establish a rapport with the prospect. You can do this while you are finding out about the assignment and exploring the background.

Usually, you have to treat each pitch as though it were a fresh campaign, so you can approach the core of the task much along the lines set out earlier in this book. But there are some crucial differences. It's a gamble. If you win the pitch, you gain some profitable business. If you lose the pitch, you have invested staff time and incurred outside costs and gained nothing. Moreover, since several agencies pitch for each piece of business, most agencies lose most of their pitches most of the time. It can be depressing.

And the prospect may not have much time for you. After all, he's got to divide his time between several agencies and get on with the work in hand. In any event, until they appoint you, he'll probably keep you at arm's length, which makes it more difficult to understand his business.

And you have current client business too. Unless the agency is carrying spare staff, you'll have to work double time.

All of this makes pitching difficult. But very few clients will simply call up an agency and appoint them. The temptation of having several agencies work for them, simultaneously and for nothing, usually proves irresistible.

Pitching is a schizophrenic business. On the surface, you are explaining your view on how the prospect can best sell more of his product. And maybe putting up some creative and media work too. So the pitch will be all about the prospect's business.

But all of this is camouflage which will often be discarded on appointment. From your point of view, the pitch is all about why your agency should have the business, rather than any of the others. Your job is to help the prospect make the right choice. That means identifying his needs and showing how your agency can fulfil them. Do you know what he wants?

One criterion may be obvious: he wants to hire an agency that can help his business grow, which means producing effective advertising. But this may not be the biggest thing on his mind, and any number of other criteria may be relevant. Here are some possibilities he may be considering.

1. Would I like to work with these people? Would I enjoy the experience?

2. Would they support me if I got into difficulty? (A friend at another agency might.)

3. Would they fit in with my company? Who at the agency would pair off with my boss?

4. Do they understand my business?

5. Are they bright enough to identify opportunities and help solve my problems?

6. Can they create an effective advertising strategy for my product? Have they done so?

7. Can they create good creative and media work? Will they do so for me?

8. Will they take my account seriously? (Will my account be a very small piece of business to them? Do they produce good work for their small clients?)

9. Do they have sufficient resources to handle my business? It may be too big for them to handle.

10. Who will work on my business? (Actually, unless agencies are carrying fat, they need to staff up when they win significant pieces of business. But the client always wants to know who he'll be dealing with.)

11. How will they charge? This is equally difficult for both sides when you don't know how much work the account will take. But unless a prospect establishes a formula before making an appointment, he risks being on the wrong end of a negotiation.

12. Do they usually produce good work for their clients? (This is about the best criterion I know. A lot of clients of agencies are

unhappy a lot of the time, but somehow the agencies hang on to the accounts. If the client wants to be happy, he had better do some research.)

13. Are they enthusiastic about my business?

If your goal is simply to win the business then you should find out how important each of these criteria is to your prospective client, and tailor the pitch accordingly. Be what he wants. But it may be that you wouldn't pay *any* price to get the business. And you may not be sure that you really want the account. In either case, there are a lot of grounds for being clear about the kind of agency/client relationship you seek.

Come out in your own colours. But make them tailor-made.

Handling check

1 Have you learned as much from the prospect as you need to?
2 Has this established the best reason why the prospect ought to come to your agency? (What is your agency's best selling proposition?)
3 And have you worked out how you can best *demonstrate* your reason?
4 Have you started a dialogue?
5 And learnt what the prospect's needs really are?
6 And how to fulfil them (if you still want to)?
7 And how your agency can fulfil his needs in a different way? (You've got to help the prospect make a choice.)
8 Will you actually ask for the prospect's business? (Or are you too shy?)

Can we have your business, please?

How should you structure your new business pitches? There is no generally known best way to do this. If there is a winning way, you can bet that the agency involved wouldn't be too keen to spread its formula around.

You need a system which is tailor-made for your prospect. How you pitch may be as important as what you say. It's an opportunity to get a message across. You need to allow the people who are involved to be at their best. If they need notes to speak, they've got to have notes.

What you need to do depends upon who you're up against. Here are some of the things you might consider in your purpose-built presentation.

1. What do you still need to tell them about the agency? You'll have had lots of opportunities to get your message across.

2. Should you send the client an advance ('leave-ahead') document to introduce the team who'll be pitching? It can go complete with photographs and abbreviated CVs.

3. Should you produce an elaborate leave-behind document? Will they read it before they decide which agency to appoint? How short should it be?

4. Is the presentation more important than the documentation? Which should influence the other?

5. What should you use to support your verbal presentation? (Slides, acetates, boards, film, sound?)

6. What is the key thing you most want them to take away from the presentation?

7. What are the main reasons why you should have their business and how can you dramatize them? (Yes, creating a presentation is a bit like creating an advertising campaign. It's an advertisement for the agency.)

8. Given these communications objectives, what is the best order for the presentation?

9. On what note should you start the presentation? As with commercials, your audience's attention is likely to be highest at the outset.

10. Where will you sit and where will they sit? Will they be able to see you and your props without difficulty? The main choices are intermingling, side to side, and end to end. If you intermingle, be careful with your notes.

11. How should you finish the presentation? What state of mind do you want them to be in when the discussion starts?

12. Will you ask them for their business or are you playing hard to get?

10 ways to present effectively

Presentation skills are a part of every account handler's regular work. It's all about clear communication, as these 10 points illustrate.

1. Know what you want to say. There really isn't much that can

be done if you are not clear about what you want to get across.

2. Know your subject in even greater depth. What you are saying should be only the tip of the iceberg. You must know why you are saying what you are saying.

3. Have a very clear and simple goal in mind. Repeat it to yourself.

4. Rehearse, rehearse and then rehearse some more. Go through it with notes and then gradually dispense with them. First time round you might try it reading from long hand, then use key words only and, once you've learnt it, do it noteless. You'll be much more effective.

5. If you are talking some way through a meeting, refer back, in passing, to any unplanned event that's cropped up.

6. Don't stick religiously to a script. If you know your script, you should be able to adapt it in the light of circumstances.

7. Keep your eyes on the audience. Give no more than a glance to slides and notes, they can't give you the business. Your audience can.

8. Visual props can demonstrate what you are saying. Don't use a visual medium as though it were a verbal medium.

9. If you are using slides, keep the audience's attention by tracking the next slide with a few words before you move on to it, for example 'As we see when we look at (click for new slide) population demographics'. And now the map is up.

10. Finally, remember that you can pause. In fact, an occasional pause helps you to emphasize a point. Like a paragraph break.

Getting it all together

As well as deciding what you need to do for the pitch, you must agree when it's going to be done and see to the organization. These jobs are the responsibility of the account handler.

You need to produce a timing plan for the pitch. And you must circulate it to everyone involved in making it happen. And you'll need to organize the presentation itself. If you can ensure the preparation is well done, your team has a much better chance of winning.

Everything has to hang together. First you need to establish your basic point of view. Then you can create a structure for the pitch. Then you can decide who will cover what, and people can start working on it.

Once you've decided what you want to say, you can work out what you'll need in the way of props. Someone needs to act as quality controller on all props, to ensure both quality and consistency between different people's efforts. The team needs to run through the presentation and agree on content before everything gets set. Then you need a period of time to make your props, before you start rehearsing properly.

After that, finalize the presentation. You'll have a lot of things to put together, even for the simplest presentations.

Presentation handling check

1   Enough agendas for everyone who's attending the new business presentation
2   Slides and/or acetates in the right order
3   Enough copies of the leave-behind document
4   Copies of any relevant agency brochures
5   Relevant case histories and advertising work
6   The storyboard/concepts and copies of the copy
7   Overhead projectors, slide projectors, carousels and screens
8   Extension leads and extensions for slide controls
9   Video tapes (VHS or U-matic) that might be needed to show the video player and TV screen
10   Production estimates, media schedules, timing plans
11   The client's brief
12   The agency's people
13   Taxis to get you there in good time
14   Spare bulbs for the projector

How to be a good loser

What do you do when you don't win a piece of business? The prospect might call you or drop you a line to convey the bad news.

The first thing to do is to thank them for telling you and, if true, say that you enjoyed the process. Then you need to know who won the business and why, and why you didn't.

It's important not to have any sort of an argument at this point. If they've made up their minds, the issue is closed. And your opportunity is to learn why you didn't win. You may be surprised. You might also be able to get the prospect to agree to pay for some or all of your out-of-house costs. It depends on their approach to business and on whether you asked beforehand.

In any event, you should wish them all success in the future. They may or may not have made the best decision for their business growth, but it's not their fault that they've chosen another agency. So no temper and no tears.

Then, it's off to see everyone who was involved in the pitch to tell them the news personally and provide a pointer to action, 'We'll have to redouble our efforts on the next pitch'. And thank them for their help on the pitch.

Once you receive the prospect's letter, write back and extend your good wishes. Don't try to score any points here.

Nobody wins all the time. And nobody likes a bad loser. Don't use your defeat to upset others, and try not to let it upset you. Simply persist.

Chapter 20

For advertisers only

Agencies attract their own kinds of clients: creative clients use creative agencies, international advertisers use agencies with international networks, planning-orientated agencies attract advertisers who believe in planning. Clients who want to run their own kind of advertising go to agencies who'll let them do so. So advertising agencies reap their own harvests. Clients have to decide how they want to be harvested.

I believe that there's no such thing as a bad client, only bad agencies. Time and again agencies will blame their clients for the kind of advertising they run. 'If only it weren't for the client', they'll say. They'll go on running second-rate advertising while quietly blaming you!

Clients could be faced, at one extreme, with an agency which insists that everything it produces is perfect and which remains impervious to the advertiser's arguments. It's either arrogant or to be prized, depending on whether it tends to be right. At the other extreme, advertisers could run into an agency which is always trying to work out what the client would like, and then providing it in 57 varieties, so that the client chooses while the agency evades responsibility.

After an agency roster reorganization, one of my clients found himself working part of the time with a well-known agency. He explained that after receiving the brief for their first job they came back with 39 concepts and sought his opinion. He turned them all down so they came back three days later with another 30! He was amazed by their lack of single-mindedness.

Clients can misbehave too. Once upon a time there was a major long-established household name, whose product was manufactured in Scotland amongst other places in the world. As well as selling its product through UK department stores, it had its own chain of shops.

Its market share was declining. It hired a team of new managers to reverse the decline – people from retail backgrounds, tough-minded cookies, and arrogant with it. The new clients instructed the agency to prepare a 'retail-style' campaign (black and white national newspapers, starbursts, with money-off coupons) based on the premise that people will only buy something if it seems cheap. The agency did so, even after a piece of research proved that housewives hated that kind of advertising for this particular product. Instead, the target audience said they wanted lots of information about the product, in a classy, preferably colour, environment. Sales continued to decline.

Eventually, after a trip round the factory which the creative team had badgered the client about for months, the agency persuaded the client to at least try selling the *product*; and a campaign ran, in colour, in women's magazines. But it was too late. The factory in Scotland had to close. And though products continue to be sold, they are all made abroad.

The point? The client had misunderstood his business. He thought he was in retailing; he should have been selling his product.

Of course, the agency should have been stronger. But they might reasonably assume their client knows more about his business than they do. This agency did, especially the account handlers. And the clients were such strong-minded people, it's doubtful if *any* agency could have persuaded them they were wrong.

The verdict could be: 'bad' agency, but very bad client. Some clients deserve to go out of business.

Equally, from an advertising point of view, there's no such thing as a bad product, only unwanted products. If the product fulfils a need, it can have first-class advertising – at the right agency. There's a notion that some kinds of products need bad advertising, financial products for instance. Yet what could be more deeply emotional than money? And when you can touch emotions, you can run emotive advertising. Many agencies blame the product's limitations for their own failings.

Still other agencies blame the size of their advertisers' budgets. Budgets are no excuse for bad advertising. True, the big agencies won't take on small advertisers because they're not geared to take on small accounts. They recognize their weakness and avoid this problem. If an agency is set up to handle small accounts, it should be set up to do the job well. And if it needs to charge an additional fee to cover the time involved, it should say so – at the outset, if possible.

10 commandments

1. Honour your agency. Let them prepare your advertising while you develop your business.

2. Expect the agency to be right more often than they're wrong, and you should back their judgement. (If they keep misjudging things, fire them.)

3. Take great care to brief your agency properly and avoid changing the brief while it is being worked on. Take equally great care to brief them thoroughly on media. If you have any prejudices, let them know at the briefing stage, not after they've done the work.

4. Don't tamper with art direction or copy, except on matters of fact. If you keep this promise, you'll probably become your agency's favourite client. And you save yourself some of the worry; the responsibility is the agency's. Don't fiddle with the media schedules either, unless you are sure they are wrong.

5. Don't allow the agency to force you to choose between alternatives. Insist on one recommendation. You are paying for their brains.

6. Allow them plenty of time to do your work. The more time you allow, the more work they can do. Don't insist on overnight advertising.

7. Tell the agency what you won't put up with. If they still do it, call them straightaway. Tell them what's upsetting you.

8. Take time out to praise them when they've done a good job. If you're really pleased tell the agency's chief executive. It'll galvanize the whole team.

9. Let the agency present their work to someone who can then approve it. Don't let them present to a whole line of staff. You are paying for both sets of time.

10. Ensure that you've agreed what the advertising is supposed to achieve, and what counts as successful advertising.

How to select an agency

Choosing the right advertising agency isn't easy, and there are many wrong ways to go about it. Consider this approach instead.

Decide which advertising you most admire. Keep a list. Make a collection of the commercials, print advertisements and so forth that you most admire. Find out which agencies produced them. Use BRAD's advertiser and agency list or the *Advertiser*'s blue book. Cross off any who work for close competition, if you are going to make this a restriction.

Consider these agencies work for other clients. Is what has attracted you just a flash in the pan or is there something consistently likeable in their work? This will help you know whether it matters much which team you get working on your account. Think about whether they would be interested in your work. What would your brand look like if it got their treatment?

Get your own files in order and prepare an advertising brief, if you are going to issue one. Drop by those agencies who've passed these tests, but try to make it no more than a handful. Minimize the notice you give to just a few days. If the agency's boss isn't around, see his deputy or whoever else they recommend. Explain that you want to hear about how they work, and that it won't be a briefing meeting.

Advertising agencies vary enormously – in their goals and in how they set out to achieve them. You should try to ensure that the agency's philosophy matches your own. How can you do so? Always start out by asking what their philosophy is. I remember once running for junior office in one of the British political parties. All three candidates, myself included, were unsure exactly what our social philosophy was. We were all asked. Two out of three had no idea. Many agencies can do little better.

Once you've asked them about their philosophy, ask them how they ensure that they live up to it. Get them to take you through their working systems. And discern their systems' pros and cons.

Then get them to take you through their work. But do it on your terms. Most agencies only show their good work, but you have no guarantee of being in their good bracket. If they're a small agency, ask to see all the work they've produced in a particular period. If they're a big agency, ask to see the client list and select half a dozen advertisers. Tell them *that's* the work you want to see. (You can apply this approach as much to your current agency as to any future beauty parade you might line up. But if it's your current agency, try to do it informally and at short notice, or they'll spend a great deal of time on the exercise, to little mutual benefit.)

You might decide to ask to tour the agency's departments and spend 10 minutes with someone from each one. You'll get much closer to the action.

Once you've completed the visits, review your first thoughts. You've probably developed your view on each agency's relative strengths.

You might be able to reduce your list further, perhaps to just one agency. If you can, you are going to save yourself and the agencies a lot of bother. You can have a businesslike discussion about resources and the agency's business terms, and meet the proposed account team. (If you don't like them, you can always ask for a different team.)

If you've still got two or more agencies on your list, you can use the pitch to help you decide. Try to set each agency the same project.

Insist on seeing no creative work. You'll expect it to evolve after appointment. Once you've appointed the agency, make it clear that you don't expect your work to be interrupted by new business pitches. After all, you didn't interrupt anyone else's work.

How should you appoint the lucky agency? When one leading advertiser decided to add a young agency to his roster he simply turned up at the agency with a bottle of champagne. That was the appointment. Do it in style and you'll galvanize the whole agency.

Chapter 21

Our acceptable face

Account handlers are advertising's ambassadors. And to judge from the press the industry has been getting, we've been less than thorough in this aspect of our work.

The advertising industry attracts both praise and prejudice in large quantities. Many people think it's a growing and glamorous industry, while others maintain that it is dishonest and parasitical. Most of the time, it is none of these. Moreover, many people are especially critical of account handlers – middle men in an industry of middle men.

To take growth first. Since the mid-1960s UK advertising has grown more slowly than the economy as a whole. And employment in advertising agencies has actually fallen. Perhaps we have become more productive. Advertising *seems* to be growing only because almost all one ever hears about is good news. Account wins, fresh budgets and promotions dominate the industry. And bad news has to be big news before people want to read about it. And you seldom hear about the client who fades away. We all put on our best faces.

What about the suggestion that advertising is glamorous? In my experience, it's not so much glamorous as high pressured. The pressure is on the industry to keep its act together and highly polished. We work to create a glamorous feeling, which is hard work.

Is the advertising industry wasteful? Undoubtedly we spend a lot of money on behalf of our clients – over 1 per cent of Britain's gross national product. Advertising is just one form of advocacy employed with relatively superficial differences by all kinds of salespeople the world over, whether they're selling products, services or ideas – and including, of course, politicians.

Is it all wasteful? I think not. Advertisers of new or better products can more quickly attract customers and achieve significant economies in production – leading to *lower* costs. And advertising's regular failure to stimulate the sales of an inferior product usually encourages clients to improve their products or withdraw them from the market altogether. Advertising increases the competitive pressure on most companies.

There's an impression about that advertising is a dishonest profession, and that we're all in some way contributing to it. To the best of my knowledge, this is not true. Of course, there are liars in the advertising business – just like any other business, or the public sector, or politics. But you really don't have to lie to get by in advertising. The truth will do nicely, thank you. Your code of ethics is implicit in your actions, and how you behave is your own personal responsibility, not that of the advertising business.

Moreover, good advertising can't keep on selling a bad product. The most you'll get is a temporary increase in sales. But it'll be at the cost of forfeiting the public's trust. They buy products in good faith. Next time you tell them anything, they're less likely to believe you. It is true that we'll put our product's best features forward, and some of the public to whom that appeals will respond. It's their choice. Admittedly, we've focused on one point without telling the whole story. But there's no deception involved in that.

The public know that we are paid to advance the cause of our clients, and they look at our claims sceptically. Contrast this with the world of public relations. In public relations, talented people are paid to influence journalists towards a particular point of view. And normally you'll never know whether or not the PR people were involved. (Actually, the best PR people are providing a service to journalists and developing or countering their prejudices.) With advertising, you know where you are in a way that you never can with an apparently independent piece of journalistic editorial. Who's trying to influence you and why is pretty clear in advertising.

There's a sense in which advertising is more representative of life. For example, in advertisements, planes usually take off and land safely, people have happy holidays and enjoy their food, and savers prosper. In editorials planes crash, holidays are often disasters, people die of food poisoning and savers go bankrupt. On average, news distorts more than advertising does. We redress the balance a little bit.

Chapter 22

Getting better all the time

A few fundamentals

1 Why are you working in advertising? (Is your answer interesting?)
2 What do you aim to contribute to advertising?
3 What's your favourite advertising campaign? Why?
4 Did it work?
5 What's the worst campaign you know of?
6 Why?
7 Why are you at your particular advertising agency?
8 What do you think of its advertising philosophy? (What philosophy?)
9 And its work?
10 What sort of advertising do you want to help create?
11 What do *you* think makes a good account handler?
12 How do you want to do your job?
13 Do you really want to work in this agency?
14 Do you really want to be an account handler? (What else could you do?)

Two Ways to Run Advertising Accounts

Advertising is a service business. Each agency is attempting to provide the best possible service to its clients, or at least a level of service that is good enough to keep it in business. It's also a specialist business. Agencies require special skills, especially if they are to do well. Most clients expect their agencies to know more about advertising than they do, just as they expect their stock-brokers to know more about the stock market.

In fact, there are really only two viable ways to run your agency accounts, just as there are basically two viable ways to run an agency. Or, indeed, to run your life. Most agencies use a mixture of the two.

At one extreme, you can simply aim to produce what your client will buy. And since satisfying the client is the only goal, you'll try to achieve it with the minimum possible amount of work, so helping to maximize the agency's profit.

In order to carry this low-road approach through you really need to find out as much as you possibly can about the kind of strategy your client would like to run and the sort of advertising he would like to see. And then you give it to him. It's remarkably simple. You ask him to buy what he wants. In the short run, it can be fairly painless, if unexciting. Better still, give your client a choice of advertising to run. You'll draw him into the process to such an extent that he may feel that he can't really criticize the advertising. He created it.

The alternative is the high road. Here, you listen intently to all that your client has to contribute, and then you think. You develop a point of view. And you put *that* to your client. This is a much riskier approach. Your client may not agree. It may take time to win him round. You may never do so.

But at the end of the day, if you know more about *how* to produce better advertising, there's always the consolation that you *will* produce better advertising. And if your client will bear with you in the short term, you may have a more solid relationship – one that's built on your expertise.

Five ways to be a better account director

1. Treat all those who work with you as though they are just as

human as they seemed to be when you were an account manager. Don't let authority go to your head.

2. Make sure you become a good listener. Before you can lead a team, you must know what they think.

3. Develop an in-depth picture of what happens and how on your accounts. Then identify the ideal in terms of income, quality of business relationship and kind of advertising. Start planning your way forward. Then act quickly.

4. Weigh your words carefully. There is much more chance that you'll be believed. Your words may well cause action, so think hard before you speak.

5. Understand the psychology of your clients. Try to know them well and to understand their aspirations, their problems and their way of looking at the world. Work out how to make them smile.

What should you read next?

Few good books have been written about advertising, and even fewer are reviewed here. Nevertheless, this book is no substitute for them. The only concern here is account handling. You can learn more from reading books about advertising, as well as learning on the job. It seems a pity not to do both.

The best all-round book I know of is David Ogilvy's *Ogilvy on Advertising*, published in 1983 by Pan Books. He's got something to say on virtually everything and he's a master of the business. He's also up to date.

How to Advertise was written by Kenneth Rohan and Jane Maas for advertisers and published in 1975 by St Martin's Press, New York. It's extremely clear and contains many valuable hints. Any good account handler should a) be able to appreciate it and b) want to know what his clients might have read. Published in Britain by Kogan Page in 1979.

Advertising, What It Is And How To Do It is an ideal introduction to the advertising business and covers all its nuts and bolts. Written by Roderick White and published by McGraw Hill in 1986.

From Those Wonderful Folks Who Gave You Pearl Harbour is Jerry Della Femina's wonderful book. Set mainly in New York and completed in 1970, it is outrageously funny and full of insight. Buy it if you can find it. Re-published by Pan Books in 1972.

Madison Avenue, USA owes its title to New York's leading street of advertising, at the time of publication. It's extremely instructive and has worn well since it was published in 1958. Written by Martin Mayer and published by Harper and Row.

The Complete Guide to Advertising was written by Torin Douglas and published by Macmillan in 1984. It's lavishly illustrated in full colour throughout and consistently professional.

Remember Those Great Volkswagen Ads? is a continuing source of joy to all who love great advertising. It's the story of Doyle Dane Bernbach's campaign for the Beetle, or bug as it became known. Published by European Illustrations in 1982 and put together by David Abbott, Alfredo Marcantonio and John O'Driscoll.

The Basic Arts of Marketing was written by Roy Willsmer and published by Hutchinson in 1976 (second edition 1984). It was re-issued in 1987 in the Hutchinson Better Business Guides Series. It's extremely useful to any account handler who wants to understand what his clients are, or ought to be, up to.

The 100 Greatest Advertisements was put together by Julian Watkins in 1949 and re-published by Dover Publications in 1959. Read it and you'll know which advertising techniques are timeless and which have dated. Published in the UK by Constable and Company in 1959.

Spending Advertising Money written by Simon Broadbent and published by Hutchinson in 1984 and *The Effective Use of Advertising Media*, third edition by Martyn Davis published by Hutchinson in 1987, both have a lot to say to anyone who wants to master the media business.

Some general management books have useful techniques and tricks to teach account handlers. Amongst those that have helped me in my work are the *One-minute Manager* series published by Fontana (so much account handling is about management under pressure); Mark McCormack's *What They Don't Teach You at Harvard Business School* published by Fontana/Collins in 1984, which provides much street knowledge about business; also *Iacocca* by Lee Iacocca, whose surname rightly spells I Am Chairman Of Chrysler Corporation of America.

There are many such books. You may have to discover your own.

Chapter 23

101 handy definitions

A (class) Higher managerial, administrative or professional people.

ABC – The Audit Bureau of Circulations. This organization audits the circulation of each advertising medium every six months. Hence, a publication may have an ABC figure of 31,000 for January–June 1987.

Account handlers – owe their job title to being individually or jointly responsible for one or more of their agency's clients, each of whom has an account at the agency. We speak of an agency's accounts when we means its clients, and of its account handlers when we mean the people who deal with its clients.

ACORN – A Classification of Residential Neighbourhoods. Typifies people by reference to the kind of area they live in, each of which is given a code. For instance, you might be trying to reach 'J34s'.

Adapt – Another version of an advertisement we already know, modified to fit a different format.

Advertise – According to the Concise Oxford Dictionary it is simply to make generally or publicly known. What is normally meant by an advertisement is a communication which is paid for by the advertiser rather than the reader or viewer (who receives it free), or the medium, which is paid to carry it.

AIDA – A copy formula mostly used in direct response advertising and mailing. The theory is that you need to get the readers' 'Attention', then generate 'Interest' in your client's product until you've created a 'Desire' on his part, then cause the reader to take 'Action', like call the company or write out a cheque.

AIRC – The Association of Independent Radio Contractors which represents independent local radio stations and approves radio scripts before they can be broadcast.

Animatic – A rough of a commercial which consists of a series of drawings which are run together as a film and are usually accompanied by a rough soundtrack, often for testing purposes.

B (class) – Middle managerial, administrative or professional people.

BARB – Broadcaster Audience Research Board, which provides television viewership reports for ITV and BBC.

Billings – The sum of money an agency spends on behalf of its clients plus the fifteen per cent spend which it usually takes for itself.

Billings equivalent – The amount of money an advertiser (or all of any agency's clients) would have to spend in order to provide the agency with the level of income it takes from its account(s) if the agency charged fifteen per cent. Hence an additional fee of £15,000 would count as a 'billings equivalent' of £100,000, even though the £100,000 was never billed.

Bleed – Advertisements that run right up to the edge of the page, as though they bleed right off the edge. 'Is the advertisement bleed or type area?'

BRAD – British Rate And Data provides advertising rate and production information on all UK media, updated monthly. In another publication, it provides details about which clients use which agency.

Brief – A brief to the creative department is a honed-down version of the advertising's objective and its strategy plus the facts needed to support both, and a definition of the target market.

Commission – Paid by media in the form of a 15 per cent discount on publicly quoted prices, which agencies do not usually pass back to the advertiser.

Concepts – A concept is the starting point of the idea that will eventually be buffed, honed, polished and fine-tuned into an advertisement. It might be a picture, or words and pictures, or just words. Creative people are solely responsible for concepts. As an account handler you can persuade, cajole and offer suggestions, while the concepts are being created.

Concept boards – Advertising ideas posted on to boards for use in research.

Corporate identity – The visual and verbal style of a company, the cornerstone of which is the company's name and logo.

Coverage – Usually expressed as a percentage of the total audience any media plan will deliver.

CPE/CPO/CPR – Cost per enquiry/order/response to a piece of advertising.

CPT – Cost per thousand people or homes reached by advertising. Used to judge each medium's effectiveness and affordability.

D (class) Semi- and unskilled manual workers.

Depth – An interview, normally with a customer, designed to elicit his views about the product.

Direct marketing – Any promotional material which reaches the consumer fairly directly, e.g. direct mail, or which is used to evoke an immediate response, e.g. direct response advertising.

Direct response advertising – Advertising that is designed to get the customer to respond immediately, whether by calling the company, clipping a coupon or redeeming a coupon at a store.

Discrimination test – Shows how many people can detect a difference between two or more products.

DPS – Double page spread made up of two facing pages in a print medium.

Duplication – The proportion of the readers of one publication who also read another.

E (class) – State pensioners, casual or lower grade workers, unemployed people.

E & OE: Errors and Ommissions Excepted – It sometimes appears on media schedules, originally intended as a legal get out.

Ear-pieces – The tiny advertising spaces at the top of the front page of most newspapers, on either side of the name.

FM – Used to indicate that an advertisement is required by the agency to be, or is, facing editorial matter rather than another advertisement.

FMCG – Fast-moving consumer goods.

Font – The complete alphabet of letters, figures and punctuation, used in printing.

Forme – Material that's ready for printing and held in a metal case.

Frequency – Measures how often an individual will, on average, be exposed to an advertisement during a campaign.

Galley proof – A proof or photo print-out of type in a single column.

Gatefold – An extra leaf folded in to extend a printed spread. Often attached to the inside front cover of a magazine.

Groups – A group discussion used to research a product, advertising or attitudes, led by an agency planner or possibly handler, or outside researcher.

GSM – Grammes per square metre, the measurements of paper weight.

Gutter – The channel running down between two pages in the middle of a spread.

Halftone – An original piece of art, e.g. a photograph, which has been broken down into small printing dots, by photographing the original through a screen.

Hall test – Research where consumers are solicited in the street and taken to a room or possibly a 'hall' for an interview. Often used when you need to interview a lot of people quickly face to face.

IA: Imitation Artwork – A high quality proof of the original artwork.

In-pro – In proportion to one another. For example, an advertisement might be blown up 'in pro' to fit a larger space of the same shape.

IPA – The Institute of Practitioners in Advertising is the body which represents advertising agencies. It can be found in London's Belgrave Square along with its advertising library.

ITCA – The Independent Television Contractors Association who you'll deal with when you want to clear a commercial script. They act on behalf of the Independent Broadcasting Authority (IBA).

ITV Association – new name for the ITCA.

Justify – Space each line of type so that both left and right ends of a column align vertically.

Laminate – An advertisement that's been coated with clear plastic to prevent it from getting damaged, or fading.

Marketing – Defined by the Institute of Marketing as being the process of identifying, anticipating and satisfying customer requirements profitably. It's also been summed up as 'selling goods that don't come back to customers who do'. It means seeing the customers' point of view at least as much as the marketer's. In marketing, the customer is always right.

MEAL – Media Expenditure Analysis Limited, an independent company which monitors advertising expenditure at rate card prices by brand, each quarter.

Mech – Or mechanical. It consists of the original artwork for a print advertisement, pasted together or with elements overlaid, or both, with a card flap to protect it.

MVO – A Male Voice-Over in a television or radio commercial, which comes from someone who does not appear in the commercial and who acts as a narrator.

Nielsen – An international market research company which specializes in retail audits allowing you to track the sales effects of your advertising campaign.

Objective – For any advertisement, this is what you want the target audience to do/think/want about the client's product.

Offset printing – Printing via an intermediary blanket cylinder.

OTH/OTS – Opportunities to hear/see. The number of times your commercial will be heard/seen on average by someone in the target audience.

Outdoor advertising – Poster and transport advertising.

Overlay – Either a sheet of clear plastic carrying part of the artwork and affixed to the board itself, or a piece of tracing paper which is flapped over artwork in order to protect it.

Page traffic – The percentage of a publication's readers who see a particular page in a publication, without necessarily noting any of its contents – usually less than the total readership.

PMT – Photomechanical Transfer. A high quality photoprint produced from a flat original for use in production or for presentation purposes.

Point – The size in which type is measured. One point is approximately 1/72″ high, twelve point approximately 1/6″ high.

Point of Sale – Publicity material or devices which are exhibited near where customers buy the goods in question.

Positioning – The way you place your product in the customer's mind.

Pre-test – Researching advertising's potential effectiveness, before it runs.

Qualitative research – Research that aims for understanding and tends to use small samples interviewed individually or in groups.

Quantitative research – Research that aims to measure and uses large samples who are interviewed in a structured way.

Register – Used in colour printing to describe the effect of printing one or more colours on top of one another.

ROM/ROW/ROY – Run of month/week/year whereby the media owner can decide when to place your advertisement within each time frame.

ROP – Run of paper. The publication can put you anywhere in their medium when this condition applies, subject to any other agreed stipulations, e.g. FM (facing matter).

Rough-cut – The first sellotaped-together version of the film with takes chosen by the film director, art director and copywriter.

Rushes – Everything that was shot at the shoot, before it is cut up and edited.

Scamp – A rough sketch of an advertisement.

Segmentation – Splitting up a market into groups by user characteristics or consumer needs.

SFX – Special sound effects. (FX means sound effects.) You come across 'SFX' on radio and TV scripts e.g. 'SFX: screech of car tyres'.

Share of voice – A brand's share of advertising impressions amongst a specified target audience.

Show-through – Where you can see the advertisement on the reverse side showing through.

Significance – A measure of the probability that a figure obtained from a sample reflects a real difference in the whole group (sampled and unsampled).

Size – Apart from the obvious, it's the name of something added to paper to reduce its ink absorbency.

Solus – A solus advertisement is the only advertisement on a page, or in a commercial break.

Split run – Occurs when you run one advertisement in half of a medium and another – usually for the same company – in another. It's often used in direct response advertising to test the relative effectiveness of two different offers, creative treatments or techniques. Here, an 'AB' split is used so that one half of the copies of the medium at each outlet carry version 'A', while the other half carry version 'B'.

Sponsorship – The act of supporting something, e.g. a theatre, by lending your name and paying a fee in order to increase awareness of your company and, perhaps, change the way customers think of you.

S/S – Same size.

Storyboard – A series of roughs of key visuals of a proposed television commercial together with a written version of the sound, pasted onto a board, for approval before shooting takes place.

Strategy – How to persuade your target audience to do/think/want whatever the objective is.

Strip in – Join one artwork image with another.

TGI – Target Group Index. An annual consumer survey of adults covering 2,650 brands, which shows levels of product and brand usage.

TMU – Type Mark Up. A typographer's instructions, marked on to a layout, for setting copy.

Tracking study – Research of the effects of advertising and marketing efforts on awareness, brand loyalty and sales over time.

TVR – Television rating. The percentage of a total audience viewing a particular commercial's appearance.

USP – Unique Selling Proposition. What your client's product has all to itself which could help it sell.

Voucher copy – The media owner's publication with your advertisement in it supplied to the agency or client, often with the invoice, as proof of the advertisement's appearance.

White goods – Electrical goods, e.g. fridges, freezers or hoovers, which are often white in colour.

Web printing – Printing using a continuous reel of paper as opposed to sheets.

Widow – A word which stands at the end of a paragraph all on its own.

Index

For Product Safety Concerns and Information please contact our EU
representative GPSR@taylorandfrancis.com
Taylor & Francis Verlag GmbH, Kaufingerstraße 24, 80331 München, Germany

www.ingramcontent.com/pod-product-compliance
Ingram Content Group UK Ltd.
Pitfield, Milton Keynes, MK11 3LW, UK
UKHW021827240425
457818UK00006B/108